GOD
THE
JOURNEY
WITH

ABINADER**BARSHA**COLONCUYJETDOVE
ERSKINEGARRIPOLIIVYJONESKLINE
L (TOUSSAINT)PARRANPENNSANTO
WASHINGTON**WEBB**WOOD

CONCEIVED AND EDITED BY DIEM JONES

Praise for God: The Journey Within

"The Mothership has landed in all of us, and Diem Jones presents a slice of our humanity by showcasing 16 distinct voices in his latest book, God: The Journey Within."
—George Clinton, Parliament-Funkadelic

"Your book is a spiritual awakening... Quite Beautiful."
—H.H. Leonards, Founder & Chair of the O Street Museum Foundation

"Thank you Diem, for your curiosity and for your desire to learn from others. Your message is clear—let us provoke thought in one another. We are created as miraculous beings that are above blindly accepting tradition and passed down beliefs. Our creator asks us
to look for Him and to have a personal relationship with Him."
—Dr. Charles Webb, Founder of Freedom Practice Coaching

God: The Journey Within

Conceived and Edited by Diem Jones

Dedication

We cannot be, without roots
...we cannot be, without branches
...we cannot be, without leaves
...we cannot be, without light
...we cannot be, without hearing
...we can only be if we allow ourselves to listen.

God: The Journey Within is a collection of reflections that is dedicated to my ancestors, my family and the spirit warriors brave enough to embrace the place at the center of it all:

Fannie J. Conrad, Charles A. Jones, Florence Francis, Albert T. Jones, Felicita Diaz, Alma H. Penn, William A. Penn, James R. Wilson & Brice Jackson

Carol A. Penn, Dima A. Jones, Keita O. Erskine, Marcia J. Hooper, Raleigh Jackson, Nika Jackson, Kiah Jackson

G.O.D. [Get On with your Do] • O.N.E. [One Never Escapes]

Diem Jones aka Drs. Fladimir MS Woo & H.M. Joy

Acknowledgements

Spirit Warriors on the Pages:

Elmaz Abinader, Debra Barsha, Frank Colón, Chuck Cuyjet, Pheralyn Dove, Keita Erskine, Francesco Garri Garripoli, Archie Ivy, Marc Kline, JD Parran, Carol Penn, Amy Shimsohn-Santo, L' Toussaint, Mona R. Washington, Kerwin Webb & Len Wood

Spirit Warriors off these pages, but on my life's Stage:

Chris Abani, Tony Browder, Kenny Carroll, Staceyann Chin, George Clinton, Bruce W. Davis, Junot Díaz, Frank Fuji, Moy Eng, Amp Fiddler, Carolyn Forché, Suheir Hammad, Jerry Hiura, Bob Knight, D. Baloti Lawrence, Clyde McElvene, Willie Perdomo, Susanna Peredo, Rochon Perry, Brenda Russell, David Spradley, Quincy Troupe, Golden Venters, Flo Wong, Bernie Worrell, Al Young

O.N.E.: God

Cover Design: Lorenzo Wilkins/SD33
Photography: Sharon Farmer

Special thanks and acknowledgement to my publisher, Cedar Grove Publishing/Rochon Perry

Introduction
by Diem Jones

Thank you for making the time.

This is a story, and every story is a story, and every story is a song…But this story and song is about the inner God, a topic I took liberty to invite 16 fellow spirit-warriors to muse upon. It was an invitation, without more guidance than a word-count range. We present a collection of poetry, prose and a play fueled by the available media canons for your muse on the topic of God: The Journey Within. What does that journey mean to you? Might you be open to be inspired to take a deeper dive? Thank you in advance.

I started my search as a young man, about eight years old, as I organized a group of friends who chose to go to different houses of worship every weekend. We planned a six-month journey, and we did everything. From temple to mosques to AME to Lutheran to Catholic to Baptist, we did it…I concluded early on that people were saying the same thing — just framed differently which sometimes led arguments as to who was saying it more properly…. [misplaced ego runs amuck across the Universe…sigh]

I looked a little deeper and said, "…well clearly there are entities or an entity that precedes us all." I synthesize that into a oneness named God. Then I read that God lies within. Surprise, surprise, surprise. Yet I was told, "You don't believe in God unless you come to church every Sunday." At that point I viewed church as a pile of bricks, and how dare they compare that to what was gifted to me inside. So, I'm of the opinion that God is within, number one. Number two, for me God is a spiritual connection, not a religious connection. Some people may disagree and that's all good… everything is good. If I have an opinion that's different than yours and we have a discussion, wow, what a joy. This is the premise and the nature of this dialogue presented by 16 authors on their journey as to what does the Inner God mean to them.

I hope that you find our collection engaging and stimulating. I am not anticipating that you will agree or disagree. What I desire is for the inner you to be on fire, to seek out a deeper place to land, a deeper core to spring from, a deeper reality to be.

So please embrace and enjoy this book, enjoy these stories, and maybe we'll have a chance one day to share our stories together. Hug a mug of joy, and remember every day, please kiss the mirror.

Diem Jones aka Drs. Fladimir MS Woo & HM Joy

Forward
Dr. Charles Webb

In a world where the predominate thought process of examining others appears to focus primarily on our differences rather than our commonalities, it is important for us all to stop and consider - we really are on the same team. We're human beings desperately trying to figure out why we are here and what exactly is our purpose. In essence, we are not each other's enemy simply because we are different. Is it not our differences and our beliefs that create curiosity within us to explore and ponder what this means? Is it not the possibilities that exist outside our conscious bubble that bring us together?

When I was asked by my friend, Diem Jones, to share my thoughts about the messages contained in "God-The Journey Within," I was touched. You see Diem and I share a special relationship that was conceived very much how this book was conceived; out of beautiful, and thought-provoking conversation.

As I read through the different authors' thoughts, I quickly discovered this book contained a montage of beliefs all regarding that longing call to interrupt our secular routine - who am I, where did I come from, and what is my purpose?

I consider myself fortunate that my curiosity got the best of me during my college years when I was introduced to a world outside of my confined ego. It was a space outside of our fourth-dimension consciousness but held the possibility to experience it here and now. For me, the search for meaning led me to the God of the Bible, YHWH.

What I learned on my journey was that I could only be introduced to alternate paths if I allowed myself to be open to them; and the responsibility of finding truth was mine. This journey also revealed to me that I had to recognize that others were also on this path, and they too would have to personally find truth. To allow others this freedom to explore is to love them. I've always felt that for those who are truly looking for the actual truth and not just their truth, God will open their eyes, their heart, and their soul to find it.

Thank you, Diem, for your curiosity and for your desire to learn from others. Your message is clear - let us provoke thought in one another. We are created as miraculous beings that are above blindly accepting tradition and passed down beliefs. Our creator asks us to look for Him and to have a personal relationship with Him.

Perhaps this book will be the catalyst to complete your journey.

Respectfully,

Dr. Charles Webb

Contents

Archie Ivy
Inside¿

Diem Jones
The Journey

Marc Kline
Blaspheme the Meme

JD Parran
God Within

Carol Penn
The God Within

Amy Shimsohn-Santo
I Am Turning a Key

Toussaint L
God is my ALL: The God in Me

Mona Washington
My Jesus Drinks Malbec

Kerwin Webb
The Essential Journey

Len Wood
Reflections of the Spirit Within

Elmaz Abinader

*Works of Mercy**

The Traditional Enumeration of the Corporal Works of Mercy
is as Follows:

To feed the hungry

> The cafeteria worker throws out the lunch my mother cannot
> afford
> To give drink to the thirsty
> We stare at the microbes floating, the dirt gathering around the
> rim
> The gas we burn wanting to drink

To clothe the naked

> When the police touched her body, her veil, and unwrapped
> her
> Lands started to burn

To harbour the harbourless

> treehouses of freeway overpasses, staking our claim on heaps
> of salvage remarkable in property,
> empty of sustenance.

To visit the sick

> Bottles like chess pieces block the view of the unopened door/
> she breathes moisture.

To ransom the captive

> The day fell into dream, taken by the state, oh youth, who die the crimes of insignificance/the insignificant

To bury the dead

> They swim madness, swallow the sea, wash up on shores, they beach

The Spiritual Works of Mercy*

To instruct the ignorant

> we forget read we forget/write/calculate
> Brain cells starve, hearts hold shallow, souls on sabbatical
> To counsel the doubtful
> The seal skin, the polar bear coat, the wolves' fur, the falcon's
> wings smear/
> the door puddle the evaporating blood

To admonish sinners

> We assemble we boycott we speak, threats are unarmed, faces
> are painted like butterflies

To bear wrongs patiently

> My slop bucket, my foil blanket, my 3 square feet, my cracked
> back, my taken child

To forgive offences willingly

> The mother in the courtroom pierces through the killer's facial
> tattoos and calls to her dead son.
> We okay ma.

To comfort the afflicted

> You have no holes, no scars we that haven't drugged, tested,
> frayed old photographs.
> wounds inside and outside the body, open to air, breathe the
> elixir of your strength to
> the coagulating blood, to the collapsing veins, to the shredded
> heart.

You are intact for now.

To pray for the living and the dead

> I have not surrendered to your doctrine, no-but ummi wi baba, I am firmly holding these words memorized and repeatednosignature saving the shells washed up to piece together this contract mercymercymercy

*The Corporal and Spiritual Works of Mercy are actions Catholics perform to extend God's compassion and mercy.

Prayer for my Garden

if I grew a victory garden for today,
I'd seed it with tears, not the sweet sorry ones, but the sweat beads
of my anger.
    grow eucalyptus and camphor
    to harden my voice, evacuate my airwaves

the starter plants, vines of words, I'd sink deep into the soil, down
into the loamy places
    where I will harvest declarations and manifestos resistances
    to brutality and excuses

the compost is the miscegenation of the history of racism and
violence, mixed well with cries of those whose deaths have not
been spoken.
    its special smoke fertilizes incentive
    to shout their eulogies to the skies

my garden remembers every one, plot speared with nametags:
George, Breonna, Ahmaud, Tony, a new crop with every season.

I am tired of these mournings, this bitter harvest.
these are grounds of ash and fire. smoldering a enraging history.
Clear the grounds, make the soil new. grow love as it burns.

When the clouds became the
opened palms of the angels.

Kareem Tayyar
Personal History

When the Clouds Became

Intending to clear smoke from my sky— forehead a canyon
history—striated walls, I enter

the earth
this anatomy

Out there, ribcage of poplars
barricade the wind, fortress the growing fields and shelter seeds
that sometimes are lost. In here, vertebrae scale chapters
of living, cracking when the plot takes a turn or goes on too long.

Out there, grapevines tangle crowns studded purple amethyst
a mission to grow without restraint--in here season sheds thistle
and bramble, a nest on the pillow impossible to comb out.

Out there, crows punctuate skylines-- a hard note in winter,
more noticeable than white winged angels
in here esophagus constricts sharps
and flats. Chords are dissolving. Song is companion.
Harder to speak, even harder to
remember.

Out there, constellations group brightly then fade as interfering
wattage blots the city, the sky; inhere tears dry from fatigue when
the creation story is rewritten in symbols follow algorithms of
abandonment.

Out there the animals are lost running on pavement, hooves torn, home lost to development where they are feared

> in here feet are flattening against attractive wood laminate,
> seeking the moisture
> of soil and sand.

Out there they tell us, what was created will heat up, burn away the stories
that we were told kneeling at the bedside
the stories are ploughed under, and nothing grows
In here, we sing into disaster a hymn
> of beginning.

Debra Barsha
The God Within

THE GOD WITHIN

Block out the sound.
Block out the committee.
Listen.

Block out the loud.
Thank the committee.
Move on.
Listen.

Still.
Small.
Inaudible.
Visceral.
Not that.
Not that.
Listen.

That.
Wander.
Focus.
Wander.
Focus.
Breathe.
Breathe.
Now.
Now.
Now.
And now.
Where?
Here.
Where?
Here.
Right here.

Gone.
Unholdable.
Fleeting.
Now.
Now.
And now.
There.
Now here.
And gone.
Seek again.

Love. Love. Love.

Frank Colón

TBTBT - Too Bad to Be True

TBTBT - *Too Bad to Be True*

"The most difficult subjects can be explained to the most slow-witted man if he has not formed any idea of them already; but the simplest thing cannot be made clear to the most intelligent man if he is firmly persuaded that he knows already, without a shadow of a doubt, what is laid before him." - Leo Tolstoy

"Faith is believing what you know ain't so." - Mark Twain

Let me begin by stating that I believe God is not dead. However, that is because I have come to believe that he was never alive in the first place!

As a child born in Washington, D.C., and raised on the island of Puerto Rico, I was always surrounded by people who invested wholeheartedly in their belief in a supernatural dimension that affected society. And, the overwhelming consensus was (and still is!) that this dimension, along with the material world in which we live, was created and ruled by an eternal, omnipotent, omniscient, and all-good entity called God.

Some of my earliest memories in this regard date back to when I was four years old and living in my parent's house in Arlington, Virginia. I recall vivid images of my uncle Francisco (my namesake) and his wife, aunt Maria (both practicing attorneys), conducting Allan Kardec-style seances down in our basement.

I was just a toddler, observing wide-eyed as my Uncle Paco spoke in tongues while other participants filled sheets of paper with "spirit writing" (psychography). Some other participants fell to the floor in a trance. At times, someone would dip their hands into the fishbowl of water placed on the center table and sprinkle everyone in the basement while conveying a message from a departed relative.

The psychographic sheets of paper, once interpreted, were summarily torn to threads and submerged in the fishbowl. All of this went on for an hour or two, depending on the number of people in attendance.

Let me tell you: it was hard to sleep at night after witnessing those sessions!

When we moved to San Juan, Puerto Rico, in 1958, I was enrolled in the Robinson School, a private Methodist institution, arguably the best school on the island. Religious services were held on Wednesdays at the school chapel, and attendance was mandatory.

At that time, my mother began taking me to church on Sundays. She became a member of San Juan's Union Church, an ecumenical, Unitarian Christian entity that conducts services based on the New Testament Revised Bible. They had a children's Sunday School where you would learn the popular Jesus stories and the hymns sung in the main chapel. I enjoyed it because the stories were entertaining and I'd find a lot of my friends from Robinson School there, as well. My father would good-naturedly drive us there and pick us up after the services.

My father called himself a Catholic - but he never went to Mass and would only step inside one of his churches once a year, on Easter Sunday morning. On this day, he would stand just inside the large church doors, holding a solemn posture, looking up at the altar and the massive cross with the body of Jesus nailed on it, and meditate with open eyes.

After about five minutes of this, feeling spiritually satisfied, he would herd us back to the car and drive us to a fast-food joint for lunch. His mood was upbeat throughout the rest of the day, feeling content with paying his sincere respects to his Catholic Creator.

My father's work as a district attorney eventually forced our small family to live in various other cities around the island. My high school years were spent in Catholic schools, the only private schools in these towns. And, as I didn't consider myself a Catholic, and these were the times of the liberal Pope John 23rd, I was not forced to attend the school's weekly service. Instead, I was relegated to an hour of "study period.", after which I would join my schoolmates for lunchtime.

This being the first time I was completely surrounded and outnumbered by Catholic people, I became curious about the differences in the beliefs they adhered to instead of what I had been learning in my former Methodist school and the Unitarian Church. To the pleasure of the nuns who taught the classes (and who would eavesdrop on me!), I dedicated that solitary study period to reading their Bible.

Until that point, I had never read anything past the pleasant stories selected for impressing children and propagating "the Good Word." But now, as I dove into the chapters one-by-one with the zeal of an inquisitor, I was first thoroughly entertained by the many accounts detailing battles and mass slaughter in the name of God.

War is usually an exciting proposition to an adolescent young man, primarily when the line between the heroes and the evil forces is clearly demarcated.

The historic old section of San Juan, Puerto Rico's capital, dates back 500 years. It was a walled city fortified by the Spanish conquistadors, as practically all the gold bullion extracted from South America and Mexico passed through the island before making the long voyage to Spain. With walls 150 feet tall and 18 to 25 feet thick, it was the most fortified Spanish city in the Americas and even withstood a long, drawn-out attack by England's Sir Francis Drake in 1595.

After reading the account of Joshua and the Battle of Jericho, I found myself imagining that if the British pirates had gathered at the base of San Juan City and played trumpets instead of using their cannons, their siege probably would have been successful!

As I read more of the Catholic Bible, I was confused and appalled at women's blatant prejudice and condemnation - the pervasive labeling them as inferior and impure. And ditto for homosexuality and for interracial relationships! There was even an instructional manual (Exodus, Chap. 21) delineating the proper procedure for treating your slaves! Also, the conspicuous transactional nature of the God from above with his subjects below seemed suspicious.

The breaking of a holy rule that could accrue a punishment was usually resolved and pardoned by publicly paying a blood sacrifice to God. And this is what I saw my Catholic friends do more mildly. After all, the basis of Catholic confession is to admit your guilt to God's representative, who will then assign you a penance to be paid, after which all is forgiven and forgotten.

I could go on for many pages about how this collection of writings - this ancient code of ethics and behavior penned two thousand years ago by ignorant people living during the Iron Age is replete from cover to cover with absurd contradictions and fantastical statements.

But I recount my youthful inquiry specifically to intellectually challenge the notions that:

1. There exists, somewhere up in the sky, an old, bearded man who is omniscient and all-powerful, and;
2. This eternal, everlasting, supernatural being is the ultimate embodiment of pure goodness.

By now, you can probably sense that besides my skepticism, I am clearly taking a stance against the monotheistic religions that rely on the Jewish and Christian Bible as the foundation of their practices and doctrines. Well, I'll go ahead and extend this to Islam, the monotheistic religion based on the Quran, which is also a descendant from the Abrahamic lineage.

My skepticism also applies to the polytheistic traditions of Hinduism, Wicca, Shintoism, Hinayana Buddhism, Santeria, and animism, to name just a few of the major players. My reason for taking this stand is that they all relish the oppression of people's behavior and thinking in one way or another.

While in college during the '70s, I was turned on to some basic principles of Hinduism via a quick adoption of the meditation techniques propagated by a young fourteen-year-old Indian boy known as Guru Maharaji. Initially, I thought his meditation methods were mysterious yet transcendent. Plus, I felt lucky to have met him in the States! After all, hadn't the Beatles (my first rock-n-roll heroes!) gone all the way to India to find themselves an Indian guru, too?

Suddenly, I felt that Guru Maharaji offered a path towards an alternative form of spirituality that didn't rely on archaic, fear-mongering "sacred" writings. My interest lasted for only about four months, though.

There was no denying the personal feeling of contentment I obtained through Guru Maharaji's meditation techniques. However, a big problem with these techniques is that they're complicated and cumbersome! And, serving to complicate Hinduism even more, is the pantheon of "gods" that populate this religion, which numerically dwarfs those of the Norse, Roman, and Nigerian mythologies combined! Oh, please!

And, besides, there was this detail of entering into an entirely devotional relationship with a barely adolescent teacher/guru - in this particular case, a fourteen-year-old Indian boy suddenly interested in the Western trappings of money, luxury hotels, private jets, and flight attendant girlfriends! These things, to me, were blurring the message of his mantra: "Jai Sat Chit Anand," which translates to "The Pure Awareness of the Eternal is Bliss."

As a musician, I was attracted to the music in the religious practices. In my junior year of Catholic high school, I frequently attended the school Mass service (again) on Wednesdays because now the parishioners could play music. It became common to perform popular songs in church with guitars and bongos.

As I was usually the "new guy" in school, I saw this as a way to increase my popularity and prestige with my new Catholic classmates. As a senior, I even joined the school choir, led by the parish priest, on account of a pretty brunette soprano I was dating

- from whom I'd steal a few kisses back in the sacristy after rehearsals. My baritone voice was serving a good purpose after all! (😉wink!)

Fast-forwarding to the '70s, I'm majoring in Political Science at the American University in Washington, D.C. I would attend classes in the daytime and play congas around the city's parks and in local bands on the weekends. My passion for drumming led me to seek out the underground Santería community, as the ritualistic beats of the Batá drums are, to me, some of the most intricately beautiful that have ever been invented.

I was fortunate to meet the eminent authority in this drumming style in 1974. The man's name was Julito Collazo, a drum master born in Havana who had come to the States in the 1950s as a dancer with the Katherine Dunham Dance Company. He took me on as his last drum disciple, observing the sincerity in my seeking spirit and acknowledging my evident knowledge of

Cuban drumming and folklore.

Due to Collazo's mentorship, I was immediately respected as an elder in this New York Latin sub-culture. Our drumming performances were religious, exalting the principal sixteen secondary deities of the Yoruba culture from Nigeria. Transplanted to the Caribbean with the Spanish slave trade, these rituals are still preserved among the descendants, and its practice has spread to various countries.

In a Santeria event, the drumming and chanting are intense, with all in attendance dancing and joining in the call-and-response singing. This can last four to six hours non-stop, with the hypnotic drumming and songs intermittently causing certain designated cult members to fall into a spirit-possession trance. When this happens, attendants take this person aside and dress them in the garbs of their patron saint/guardian angel. Once in costume, the possessed individual returns to the party to bless his followers and offer personal advice and divination.

I worked in this underground ministry as a ritual drummer under Julito Collazo's guidance from 1976 through 1981. When I felt the urge to move on, Julito simultaneously retired from active drumming and transitioned into the role of Babalawo/priest. His parting advice was, "Go out into the commercial world and expand your horizons artistically and philosophically beyond this small cult community that you've temporarily adopted." And so I did.

I've told you a bit of my personal story to illustrate how I'd been diligently looking for a direct connection to a Supreme Being through most of my younger years. At this present stage of my life, now that I'm seventy years of age, have I found this connection?

My answer is: No.

You could immediately retort with the question: "Were you searching in the correct place - in the right direction?" "Were you seeking a connection with the appropriate spiritual attitude?" "Did you surrender your ego, Frank, and seek to experience God (or Jesus, or Ganesh, or Changó) deep in your heart?!"

The quick answer is: Yes! Through all these previously described authentic and immersive experiences, I was open and willing to believe and accept them all as genuine. But I wanted to have faith based on confirmable evidence instead of a blind acceptance of the myths and commandments preserved, protected, and dictated by authoritative hierarchical figures.

Wouldn't this be the typical attitude for a person in the twenty-first century?

As I use the word "faith," I know that the type of evidential belief that I was looking for goes smack against the Cambridge Dictionary's definition of the word, which states that it is:

"A strong belief in God or in the doctrines of a religion, based on spiritual apprehension rather than proof."

Sure enough, in my youthful and adult discussions with nuns, priests, gurus, Santeros, and other ministering spiritual leaders, we have always come to a junction where, according to them, the unexplainable "should be accepted based on faith." To all these representatives of cult and organized religions, my lack of "experiencing the Divine" was attributable simply to my lack of faith. According to these people, the problem was with me and not their systems.

But, while I was open-minded about the existence of something other-worldly that might clarify the universe's mysteries, I've never found any actual scientific proof for this. To stand up to scientific scrutiny, a concept must triumph in controlled testing and yield the same result no matter how challenged it is. It can't simply be accepted as fact because it presents a charming and pleasant theory.

Nor should it be accepted and propagated because of the psychological comfort it may afford. Much less should it be obeyed under the threat of punishment or execution!

I've often wondered: why is it that when the subject is about religion and God, considered by millions to be the eternal, magnanimous (albeit jealous!) Creator of all that exists, we must immediately and voluntarily suspend all intelligent critical thought and simply accept His existence and authority - for our own good (and safety!)? Where's the logic in this? (And, lest I forget - intelligent reasoning and scientific analysis must all be voluntarily surrendered concerning this subject, as well!)

Personally, I'm not sitting on the middle of the fence in my views, affording the possibility of the existence of God, or Santa Claus, or the Tooth Fairy a fifty-fifty chance of proving themselves. I stand my ground in asserting that I've never been given sufficient reason to believe that any myths mentioned above are accurate.

Most adults eventually outgrow and move forward beyond our childish enthusiasm for Santa. However, influential figures and personalities in a society constantly reinforce the adherence to the doctrines of organized religion upon the minds of children and people throughout their entire lives.

I find it especially ludicrous to affirm that a baby is "born a Lutheran," "born a Jew," or "born a Hindu!" A baby comes into this world devoid of any political or religious views. They biologically react to stimuli on instinct alone until the time comes, years later, after which they begin to understand language and formulate their own simple thinking into understandable words. And, most often, they eventually first adopt the religion of their parents. That's how it works in most cases.

Think about this: had you been born in Saudi Arabia, the religion you would have inherited (by law!) would be Islam, and your Divine Ruler would be Allah. You would fall into these beliefs not by choice but totally by accident!

And, in the case of Islam, please don't ever dare to question the validity of this imposition, much less in public, for the penalty for apostasy in orthodox Muslim countries (such as Saudi Arabia, Somalia, Mauritania, Yemen, Bahrain, Qatar, Iran, U.A. Emirates, Uzbekistan, Kyrgyzstan, and Tajikistan) is death by execution. Your death sentence could be administered by the government or a mob, depending on the country.

In the Muslim countries of Malaysia, Brunei, and Indonesia, apostasy carries a prison sentence. A person accused of converting another away from their faith in Islam is a crime leading to immediate arrest and imprisonment in Morocco, Turkey, Libya, Algeria, and Western Sahara. A Muslim questioning their faith or changing their religion in Egypt, Jordan, and Oman can be separated from their family and lose custody of their children.

However, the final word and superseding the aforementioned

local interpretations of Islamic jurisprudence is the Hadith. This compilation of anecdotes of the Prophet Muhammad's words and deeds is considered the linchpin of Islamic culture. Serving to back up the teachings of the Quran, the Hadith doesn't quibble in sentencing all apostates to immediate death by execution!

As a musician, I've traveled through the Muslim countries of Uzbekistan, Turkmenistan, Azerbaijan, Kyrgyzstan, Malaysia, Turkey, and Indonesia. Most of these tours were sponsored by the

U.S. State Department in conjunction with The Kennedy Center's "Jazz Ambassadors" program.

It's a selection process during which each musician candidate must audition and be vetted by State Dept. officials. We are then briefed as to what to expect as far as the social norms of each country.

There are also significant personal and group safety, health, and nutritional considerations when traveling through these countries, which we are also lectured on before embarking.

One of the points strongly emphasized by all the U.S. Government officials was: "Please keep your personal religious philosophies to yourself! Do not practice your faith overtly in public, and refrain from sharing your own religious views with anyone!"

An example of this would be: "If you're inclined to kneel and pray 'Hail Mary' or chant 'Om' in the Lotus position in your hotel room, do so very quietly! Do not let the adjoining room inhabitants or the housekeeping attendants hear you! Muslim Shari'ah Law prohibits the influencing of a Muslim devotee towards considering a different philosophy or questioning his own faith in Allah. Should you disregard this, both you, the influencer, plus the person who listened to you can be taken into custody and punished severely."

On my first tour of Indonesia with the Manhattan Transfer Band, government officials were present during the band's sound-check in Jakarta. While the band played, testing mic and instrument levels, this Muslim Morals Committee appeared visibly uncomfortable, conversing in an agitated manner while pointing to the stage.

It took no more than ten minutes before an interpreter approached the band's road manager aggressively demanding an immediate stop to the rehearsal. The apparent problem was my very long and curly (past shoulder-length!) rock-n-roll hair. Compounding the offense was my lack of a beard! A sign of the times, I did look like I'd just stepped out of a 1989 MTV heavy metal video shoot! The problem was that Indonesia's religious laws prohibit "a man with a shameless female appearance" from performing in a public event.

After a lengthy discussion, it was agreed that I could perform. Still, I had to tie my hair back in a bun, wear a baseball cap (a turban was suggested!), and position myself behind the band's drummer, almost totally out of view from the audience!

Furthermore, in no discreet terms, it was advised that I should not walk the streets of Jakarta with my hair loose, resembling a rock star! I was warned that my appearance could provoke Muslim men into attacking me. And, should this happen, I would have no legal recourse for filing a complaint.

Most Christians plus Conservative and Reformed Jews are unaware that apostasy is also prohibited in their Bibles. This is a canonical fact that is, nowadays, ignored by both of these churches! Did you know that the Old Testament book of Deuteronomy stipulates death by stoning for a close friend or family member (spouse, daughter, son, or mother) who would secretly seduce you into considering a different line of worship?

Even Jesus, whose mission was, in part, to assure the forgiveness of all sins upon a person's sincere repentance, draws the line at blaspheming the Holy Spirit. Do this (Mark 3:29), and you've forever forfeited your ticket to Heaven!

Had you been born in Southwestern Nigeria during the last century, your family would have instructed you in the ways of the Yoruba religion. The tribal Yoruba religion believes in a supreme creator of the universe called Olodumaré who lords over approximately 400 lesser gods called Orishas ("saints") and spirits ("angels"), but who is too divinely essential to be dealing with the mundane affairs of human life. Olodumaré, therefore, has relegated his lower court to interact with humanity.

A very popular Orisha ("Santo") goes by the name: Changó. As the legend goes, he was a womanizing warrior king whose body floated up to Heaven upon his natural demise.

The Yoruba ideology is rife with taboos, superstitions, and ritualistic blood sacrifices, all performed to obtain desired favors or appease the many divinities. (I ask the Catholic reader if this, at all, sounds familiar?)

Why do I take the time to share my views with you? After all, don't some religions still have positive elements to contribute to the wellbeing of society? Don't most people need Divine Supervision - Heavenly Security Cameras aimed at Earth - to coerce humanity to toe the line and tailor its behavior according to the norms of a civilized religious society? Millions of people sincerely believe that without God or Allah looking down on the world and taking names, humankind would consist of constant chaos, violence, rape, and (God forbid!) blasphemy!

I simply don't buy this, as human history has shown us that most mass violence has occurred throughout the centuries in the name of God! The burning of witches in Salem, Massachusetts, the wars of the Crusades in Europe and the Middle East, the Spanish Inquisition (with its proliferation of torture artifacts invented to "facilitate" interrogations), the bombing of Pearl Harbor, Hawaii, and the destruction of the World Trade Twin Towers in New York are all examples of sincere individuals collectively acting to eradicate opposing philosophical views. All in the name of God, Jesus, the Divine Emperor of Japan, and Allah.

You may argue that most of humanity is not enlightened enough to act morally on their own and, therefore, intrinsically needs a divine code of ethics and conduct. Where would we learn moral behavior without a holy, authoritative lord dictating the rules?

This argument to me is overly simplistic, insulting, distasteful, and totally condescending. C'mon now! How patronizing can you be? The evolution of secular moral philosophy begins with the teachings of Socrates (born around 470 BCE), who, above all, emphasized rational inquiry. His legacy continued through his disciple, Plato, who later taught Aristotle.

Their inquisitiveness concerning the activities of the natural world components was never extinguished. And running concurrently with these free-thinking Greek philosophers were the Roman Stoics and Epicureans.

The Stoics of ancient Rome believed that people needed to cultivate the four cardinal virtues of justice, prudence, fortitude, and temperance to attain a prosperous and meaningful life. They thought this was possible without answering a Higher Authority and proved it true through their own example.

Epicurean thought is similar, encouraging the study of philosophy for achieving a happy and contented life, free of pain and fear. Epicurus taught that mankind's mental afflictions and emotional maladjustments resulted from the widespread, socially acquired fear of dying painfully. Believing that physical and spiritual death were both, indeed, final at the moment of your demise, then there was no logical motive for a further uneasiness about an imagined extended outcome.

It's not like the concept of an alternative and secular source for morality is new. These guys lived and disseminated this point of view more than a couple thousand years ago!

Religions confuse people by fomenting that their particular doctrines and commandments automatically equal the desired moral conduct applicable to all under their broad ministerial umbrella. Really?

Think about it. By modern social standards, a person who lived his life acting out all the edicts written in these ancient, obsolete books would be rightfully considered to be a dangerous psychopath.

Seventeenth-century philosopher and mathematician Gottfried Leibniz expounded the hypothesis that everything in nature, animate and inanimate, possesses a mind of its own. To him, there was a universal consciousness able to perceive its own surroundings and its relation to the environment. While he didn't totally discard the notion of a Creator, he stated that belief in the supernatural should be substantiated by rational analysis instead of being justified simply by faith alone.

Jumping ahead to the eighteenth century brings us to

philosophers David Humes from Scotland and Immanuel Kant from Germany. From Humes comes the notion that humans are generally endowed with the foundations of ethics and morals, these being embedded deep in our desires, emotions, and feelings - in our "passions," as he was fond of saying.

Considered to be what we would label today as an agnostic, Humes both challenged the arguments of his era for God's existence while simultaneously pondering the characteristics of such an omniscient entity, if it, in fact, did exist. However, he rejected the dictates of what he termed as "religions revealed from above" and then codified by humans according to their own desires, intellectual limitations, and personal prejudices. Ultimately, he concluded that scientific reasoning couldn't be stretched into eventually leading to any form of deity.

From Kant, we get the notion that our moral norms should originate from plausible ethical allegations, which should then be tested and evaluated for their truth and validity. Based on these tests, such claims could and should be modified and improved to best serve the interests of society as a whole.

This involves scrutiny on a case-to-case basis to arrive at the collective's agreed notion of right and wrong. An agent of power such as a government would then objectively ensure the adherence to these universally accepted rules of moral comportment for the greater good of collective society.

My purpose in sharing my views here on this subject is not to attack those who enjoy their religious faith. Everybody should be free to believe whatever they desire. This is my main point! My reason for writing this text is to stimulate free thinking. I respect society's public laws, but I despise those who attempt to restrict or curtail my freedom of speech, thought, and deed under the guise of religious doctrine.

As Americans, we tend to feel that the built-in constitutional separation of church and state has guaranteed our immunity from religious intrusion in our daily lives. The United States also purports to uphold freedom of religion and thought, with the right to express your own beliefs or non-beliefs, so long as this doesn't infringe upon the rights of others. And complementing these concepts is the prohibition of discriminating against anyone based on personal beliefs.

Notwithstanding, at the state level, there are still laws on the books which prohibit specific sexual practices (even behind closed doors in the privacy of one's home!), the residue of religious taboos, and discriminations.

Likewise, certain books are routinely banned from school and public libraries, as some local boards of education and municipal councils deem them inappropriate for students. Recently the book "Maus," by cartoonist Art Spiegelman, has suffered this censorship. However, the same fate was awarded to "Huckleberry Finn" by Mark Twain, "Fahrenheit 451" by Ray Bradbury, "The Color Purple" by Alice Walker, and "Harry Potter and the Sorcerer's Stone" by J.K. Rowling, to name just a few.

But are we Americans indeed allowed to be free in thought? Would we elect an openly atheist individual to the office of President anytime soon? Since there are still eight states (Arkansas, Maryland, Mississippi, North Carolina, Pennsylvania, South Carolina, Tennessee, and Texas) that legally prohibit atheists from holding public office (and, in some cases, from testifying in court!), I don't think so.

In conclusion, I re-state that the invitation to participate in this compilation book, "God: The Journey Within," sparked my desire to share my life experience and current thinking to stimulate the reader's own thoughts on this subject. I believe that I've made it clear that I don't think there is a god within us, nor are there gods or spirits out there in the stratosphere.

Science has explained that thunder is not Thor throwing his hammer across the heavens. Science has also clarified that epileptic seizures are not evil demons entering a person's body. And earthquakes and their consequent tsunamis are not divine punishments from God but result from the planet's shifting tectonic plates. We've got that figured out…right?

The progress of science relentlessly debunks more and more ancient superstitions, always moving humanity towards an improved perception of the natural beauty and elegance of the universe. Using critical thought, scientific study always admits what it hasn't deciphered yet.

When science encounters an unknown frontier, it doesn't take the easy way out, lifting its arms up to the sky, declaring, "Well, since I don't have an immediate answer, this phenomenon must surely be attributed to the work of Allah! InshAllah!"

Science continues evolving the technologies which will expand and fine-tune our understanding of our vast universe. And, as today's preeminent astrophysicist, Neil deGrasse Tyson, has said, "The good thing about science is that it's true whether or not you believe in it."

Will science eventually give us all the answers to the mysteries of our world and the universe we're part of? Maybe. Maybe not.

And - I'm ok with that.

Am I still searching for a direct experience with the supernatural? Do I suffer from the realization that the here and now are all that exists? Am I disillusioned from the understanding that to expect an afterlife in an entertaining and enjoyable divine theme park in the company of the Abrahamic God is pure silliness and will not occur? Quite frankly, my comfortable answer to all these questions is: Not at all.

On the contrary, to have discarded these superstitious theories has liberated me to make the absolute most of my life! For, in place of awarding importance to guilt and atonement, I focus on my personal responsibility to maximize my life's productive potential in ways that create happiness for myself and my loved ones. And, if my attitude and consequent actions advance the progress of humanity as well, then I believe I'll be scoring a double-whammy!

I would encourage you (and it does require courage!), to never give up and take the easy road. Please question everyone and every system which requires your compliance and blind faith in the mysterious "ancient, sacred ways" which justify themselves with circular arguments and rationalizations. The burden of actual proofs on the supernatural believers, not on the skeptical thinkers of the world.

Extraordinary claims require extraordinary evidence, which must stand up to scientific investigation. Scientific analysis has consistently explained mysterious phenomena happening in the objective reality of our marvelous material world.

I can't come up with one example of any church debunking a scientific discovery and successfully reverting the deductive diagnosis back to its archaic mythical religious assertion.

If you can come up with one example of the reversal of science in favor of a fairy tale, please enlighten me.

I'm all ears!

Chuck Cuyjet

Living Life Consciously

Living Life Consciously

"Purpose is the essential element of you. It is the reason you are on
the planet at this particular time in history. Your very existence is
wrapped up in the things you are here to fulfill."
Chadwick Boseman

I wake up and the first thought and first sound that passes
through me is "Thank you."

I think of it as my morning prayer which is offered in sheer
gratitude for another day. Something that has not been given to
several people I've known and loved over the years, two in the
last few months. I'm at that stage of life where it's natural to have
people that have cared for me and been in my circle of compassion
and love pass on. Their love remains a blessed memory and still
instructs many aspects of my life. Without giving it too much
thought I realize that I go through life guided by both conscious
and unconscious habits and beliefs. Waking up to a new day I
certainly don't think of any of this, I just take a breath and exhale
my thanks. But while my approach to the present still contains my
sincere thanks for breath it also holds something much simpler.

It is the breath itself.

I take it in consciously and feel it course through my body,
awakening each cell to awareness. I exhale that first breath with
the words 'thank you' and offer the promise of reaching for each
moment granted to me with relish, gratitude, and enjoyment. My
second breath comes with a question: "What will my lessons be
today?"

Some days it's, "What can I do today that will be meaningful?"
But always it's some sort of question. I take subsequent breaths
and exhale them in a quest to see if I can find the right question or
questions for my day. But I never let the search obscure the clarity
before me. Most times the questions become clear as the day goes
on.

And life is clear when I stay present in the moment, even the painful ones. They perhaps ask the best questions and offer the best lessons. I feel the pain, sometimes the panic, and I remind myself to calmly breathe and be in the moment. I still feel whatever pain there is, whatever panic that arises but those feelings are less than what I am. I have the same approach for those delightful, pleasant moments as well, delving into the pleasure of them but reminding myself that they are momentary.

The moments most important to me are those I share with others, the stories we create together. The people that mean the most to me are those who share the sacredness of the moment. Dear friends and strangers who pass by on life's sidewalks and roadways. Holding sometimes just a glance for a second but offering their complete presence to me and the world they contribute the highest coin to our treasury of life, themselves.

At night, I see what questions I have attempted to answer, what experiences I've learned from, and what I may have offered of value. Regardless of my summation as I find just the right position under the covers I take in a deep breath and utter aloud my night prayer, "Thank you!"

We all go, leaving footprints, tears, and, hopefully, some smiles behind along our paths. The trick, I think, is to flavor the walk with love. I try to think of my Catholic schooling when I want to reflect 'walking with love'. I'm retired now.

But I've been a middle school teacher and basketball coach, a university career counselor and employability skills instructor, a leadership and executive coach. The easy summation, for me anyway, is to say I've led a life of service to others.

What I find interesting is that I don't think of God or religion in any of this. I'm not a religious man. Aside from my Catholic schooling I also had a strong influence from my mother's Baptist family. My maternal grandfather was an ordained minister and while he had passed before I was born his presence in the family was still very strongly carried on by my grandmother. My father's family is fiercely Catholic.

I got the old book and the new book in spades you could say. I also read from other faith traditions and was greatly influenced by

Rabbi Hillel who reportedly said that beyond the Golden Rule, 'all else is just commentary'.

Just commentary...I'm not saying that the commentary is worthless...just the opposite, it...all of it, is worthy of reading and deep study. But in all that I have studied in the contact with the page and in the essence of what I have read, it pales in comparison with the many faces of God I have seen in the people I've met, the actions of love and compassion I've witnessed...in those lovely places on the earth I've visited and felt awe and wonder at such sublime beauty.

There I have experienced God.

So, I wonder, do you have to be religious to believe in a God? And if one does believe in something a Christian calls God, is it sacrilegious for that same person to say that there's no way any of us can be that certain of whatever scripture we may follow? After all it is called 'faith'...a belief in something not seen.

I'm not a religious man. I believe that there is a higher power and that we...all of us...are reflections of that thing some of us call God. I've had way too much experience NOT to believe. But don't try to tell me that I should/must believe as you do. God is attributed with many powers, omnipresence being one of them. God's message to humankind is reflected in the Vedas, the Torah, the Bible, and the Koran...the sutras of Buddhism and, in my very humble prayer of "Thank You" that I utter every morning and each night.

Just a thought, but like I said, I am not religious. I wonder why anyone would tell me I need more. I wonder why people claim that the word they have is better, more sufficient, than those two..."thank you"...and I must say, that ever since I started my meditation practice, I've come to understand that's when whatever God there is speaks back to me...when I am quiet, placid, and still... not attaching to any word, no doctrine, no dogma...just spirit. And my breathing, in and out, with no attachment to what my mind might be processing. Reaching without effort to the calmness within, to the divine within.

"If the only prayer you ever say in your life is thank you, it will be enough."

Meister Eckhart

Pheralyn Dove

Way Too Polite

Way Too Polite

Vexed. Evil. Spirits.

My angels and my demons are warring against each other,
fighting over the very possession of my soul. During a
particularly fierce battle, my demons prevail. My angels are
forced to retreat. I am vulnerable, defenseless: sinking, sinking,
sinking: further into an ever-deepening chasm.
Swimming in quicksand:

feet, ankles, calves.
knees, thighs, hips.
torso, chest, neck.
mouth, nose, eyes.
brows, hairline, head.

I am immersed in muck.

I am utterly worthless, morbidly sad.

I plummet even further into the pit, tumbling down the
ominous hole.

Earth Mother Angel Contemplating

Last night I had "my dream." The dream I dream sometimes
when I am asleep. The dream I dream sometimes when I am
awake. The dream sequence where my angel comes to teach me
about me. The "spiritual being" part of me. Not this earthly
person enclosed in my physical body. My angel comes to help
reveal my true essence. The real me. The part of me obedient
to God. Earth Mother Angel floats around her habitat in the
heavens, surveys her surroundings.

Billowing clouds gently embrace her, warm her, support her,
nurture her. She gathers up her skirts and shawls of mauve,
lavender, purple and powder blue. She flutters her silvery dove-
grey wings, feels the vibes, begins to focus her attention on me.

She has visited me often over time.
But she's never there when I sink into the hole.

Self-Esteem (Or Lack Thereof)
For someone who clearly has intelligence, an education, skills,
creativity, a list of accomplishments, the obvious question
begs: Why do I feel this way? The answer? I don't know. I just
don't know. (Or if I do know, deep down inside, I am afraid
to expose trauma I experienced but am not yet willing to deal
with. I am afraid to seek professional help although I know I
should.)

But Why?
I have this poem where I write about walking around
looking like "a million dollars," yet deep down inside feeling
"worthless." I am being thrashed about from one crisis to
the next starting off with my divorce. Then I lose my job.
I get another job (paying less than half the amount I need
to cover my monthly household expenses, let alone food
and transportation.) Then I lose this job too. My car gets
repossessed. I am so behind in my daughter's tuition payments
at Howard University, they are calling and sending letters,
threatening to send her home. My gas gets shut-off. I am in
this house with no freaking hot water, no use of my gas range.
My house goes into foreclosure. It is listed for Sheriff's Sale.
I am embroiled in a court case over a property settlement on
the house (Yes, the same house that is now in foreclosure).
"This Old House," is how my daughter and I refer to it, how
we lovingly refer to our home. Our home has "good bones,"
but it needs work; it needs major work and living in here is a
challenge from day to day; a pure challenge! For the most part,
the front porch, living room, dining room, kitchen, even the
bathroom and front bedroom are nicely appointed, clear of
clutter....but don't open any of those closets! Don't go behind
any of those closed doors! Don't peek into any of those
drawers!

Clutter, overwhelming clutter. And the leaks! Oh my God!

The leaks in this house. The worst! Leaky faucets. Leaky pipes. Leaky roofs. But this is our home!!!! Our palace. I absolutely adore "This Old House." I am bereft over the thought of losing her.

(I realize I am in this situation through nobody's fault except my own.) I blame myself. How could I be so stupid to put myself in this situation? Proves how worthless I am. The levee broke! Here comes the flood. I am drowning.

Ironically, sometimes just over my shoulder I glimpse this fleeting sense that I am protected. I wake up overwhelmed by three threatening court judgements hanging over my head. But as I look up at the ceiling from my bed, I consciously give thanks for still being here. I become slightly aware of a shift happening. The wave of light quickly passes through me. Then my thoughts return to this bleak existence.

Freaking Out

Well, I must tell you. While I am freaking out with loathing and depression over my overall worthless self, I am also freaking out about turning 50 next year. Actually, panic-stricken would be a more apt description. Feeling like I have squandered my life; feeling like I have no way out.

Countdown: less than two years away. While I am going through the broke-money blues, the

no-work, no-food blues, the no new shoes blues - I don't know where I thought I would be at this point in life, but I certainly did not think I would approach 50 still fraught with the same insecurities I struggled with at 40 years old, 25 years old, 13 years old, 7 years old!

And How?

Night after night I am possessed by graphic thoughts. Nasty, nagging thoughts. But sometimes I fall asleep and wake up to discover that I have been dreaming. Dreaming about my angels coming to rescue me.

Redemption
I wake up one day and realize I have gotten way off my
running schedule.

I trek over to Valley Green - pace into a nice, steady run. The
melodies of the Wissahickon Creek serenade me in perfect
harmony, the water flowing with the rocks, the wind, the trees.
Miraculously, I let go. The glory and wonder of being out in
nature calm my vexed spirit.
Cooling down after my run. Feeling exhilarated, exuberant.

Blessed Assurance
My actual turning point comes somewhere around 18 months
prior to my 50th birthday. I am working a day-job as a grant
writer for the Philadelphia School District. While the benefits
are   good, the pay is embarrassingly low. (My salary is so
paltry I qualify for the government's Earned Income Tax
Credit, a program designed exclusively for the working poor.)

So here I am, at the 24-hour copy center. It is a weeknight. It
is after midnight. I am printing out poems I typed up earlier
that evening. I methodically collect them up - stack the pages
into neat little piles. I allow my mind to wander. Suddenly, I am
stunned by this absolutely orgasmic epiphany. So what if I'm
feeling worthless because of what I haven't done up until now!

So what if my roof is leaking. So what if I am forced to
make up excuses and leave work immediately at the sign of
an imminent downpour. So what if I still have some of my
books and files stored in milk crates I've been lugging around
since college? So what if I haven't run a marathon? What are
my possibilities now! Didn't the Lord deliver me from that
whole court battle over my home? Am I not living proof that
miracles can happen, even with no job, three court-ordered
judgments and a foreclosure working against me? Didn't the
Lord give me grace, straighten out my mortgage mess and
place me in a union job with benefits and the potential for a
pension, a job where I get paid to write all day, polishing up my
technical writing chops?

Didn't the Lord make a way for me to stay connected to my artistic craft, and continue to perform "Little Girl Blue," my one-woman show, even though I am tied to a day job? And my angels. . . aren't they still giving me inspiration to write poetry and essays and teach classes? What about my health and fitness? And my beautiful daughter? What about my parents and my siblings and my extended family and our amazing network of friends? Our village. Our generations-deep chosen community. Didn't I wake up this morning? What about today's sunrise? And yesterday's sunset?

Right then and there, I decide to train for the 2005 Philadelphia Marathon as my 50th birthday gift to myself. A few weeks after that, on the first Sunday in May 2004, I lace up my sneakers at the starting line of the Broad Street Run. I complete my personal best 10-mile race.

I do not look back.

Over that summer of 2004, I am inspired to start going to church. I begin to worship frequently at Enon Tabernacle Baptist Church with my dear Sister Friend, My Spiritual Sister, Joyce. She happily encourages me every Sunday. (Joyce has been praying for my salvation for years.) On that first Sunday in October of 2004, a day or so after my 49th birthday, with Joyce holding my hand and tears rolling down my face, I take that walk down the aisle to the altar. Joyce lets go of my hand. Rubs me across the shoulders, pats my back and leaves me there.

I lay it all down. I surrender.

When 2005 arrives, I do not feel so desperate and alone and down on myself. As the year progresses, I stay true to my running schedule. My intellectual and creative pursuits pick up, in tandem with a hefty pay raise at the School District. (Good riddance to the Earned Income Tax Credits.) My director friend Mel Donaldson produces me in "Little Girl Blue" at Freedom Theatre for the Philly Fringe Festival. On the eve of my 50th birthday, September 30, 2005, I am ever so grateful to find myself on stage at the University of Pennsylvania's Annenberg Center, performing as the guest poet, with guest saxophonist Odean Pope, band leader and bassist Tyrone Brown, harpist Gloria Galante and the rest of the members of the amazing group "Kusangala." Six weeks later, on November 20, 2005, I get in The Philadelphia Marathon starting line up on Benjamin Franklin Parkway.

The gun goes off.

I hurl into motion.

I do not stop until the deed is done.

26.2 miles later, I give the victory sign as I cross the finish line.

My First Marathon!!!!!
Exactly one year later, I say my prayers as I peer over the rim of the Grand Canyon overwhelmed by this amazing force of breath-taking natural beauty. I thank the universe for this truly remarkable life I live. I am still on a natural high from my performance on stage a month earlier in Paris, at the 2006 Jazz a la Villette Festival, along with Khan Jamal, Monnette Sudler, Byard Lancaster, and all the phenomenal cats in the "Sounds of Liberation Orchestra." I reflect and say, "Yeah Girl, you screwed up." (Big time!) "But even so, you didn't do so bad for your first half century after all."

Today my spirit is full of praise, gratitude. The broke-money blues, the leaky roof blues, the woe is me blues – all distant, distant memories. Broken bits and pieces of a forgettable past.

Way Too Polite
I shudder as I think about those awful low points in the

valley. Before my salvation, my redemption. Flailing. Fighting fatal thoughts. Falling through crevices. Possessed by graphic thoughts. Pills? A gun? Jump in front of the subway? Jump off the Platt Bridge?

Yet the more I would think about the actual details, the more I concoct scene after grisly scene in my deranged imagination, the more I become convinced that self-inflicted dead bodies are just too messy. (After all - there is the fundamental question of manners.) I could never be that rude. A properly raised Negro female of my ilk is just too considerate to intentionally leave a gruesome dead body for somebody else to clean up. Yes, I admit. Before God's grace turned me around, I was contemplating suicide. But in the end, not only did I realize I had faith, I also realized I am simply way too polite to kill myself.

~. ~. ~

Excerpted from Paradoxes: The Book by Pheralyn Dove
Publication Release October 1, 2022

Keita Erskine

At Night I Don't Pray

At Night I Don't Pray

Sometimes, it takes saying the thing out loud.

Sitting alone in a neighborhood bar a few years ago, a patron noticed my crucifix. This man was soaked in whiskey and ready to preach, so I let him, until he asked if I believed in God, to which I responded, "I'm not sure."

Flabbergasted, he pointed at the piece dangling from my neck. The jewelry was, after all, his whole reason for preaching to me in the first place. He told me he felt comfortable with me because he felt I was a true believer. He felt he could share in the Gospel because I was clearly a follower of Christ.

Except I wasn't, am not, and won't be in the future. I told him the crucifix was a family heirloom, passed from my maternal grandfather to me, and while Papa may have been the true believer the man was looking for, he didn't go to church very often and mostly kept his faith to himself. He made no attempt to raise me in the church and I never really understood why he left me that piece, but it made me feel close to him so I kept it.

The barfly ordered shots for us and the bartender. We toasted Papa and he left, awash in booze, while I sat there drowning in existential crisis; I wasn't sure?! I'd self-identified as many things, from Baptist to Quaker to Agnostic, but all of them were grounded in certainty. My first name means "one who has faith" and I always took that literally. Whether it was God or the Mets, my faith was dogged and permanent. It was always something I was proud of.

This man had pressed me quite gently; all that faith in the Almighty had wavered like willows in a hurricane. I wasn't sure?! What the fuck was that?! But, while I sat there, taking stock of my life, I realized this uncertainty had not appeared out of nowhere. In fact, it had been brewing for quite awhile. By the time this barfly ambushed me, I was several years removed from attending church regularly, well over a decade since I picked up a Bible to do anything other than kill a roach, and maybe twenty years since I last prayed unprovoked. I'd been going through the motions of faith. I lost whatever thread connected me to the churches of my youth; I bristled at the idea that I should practice any sort of religious ceremony.

And yet, I hadn't said, "no, I don't believe." I paid my tab and walked out into the cold November night. At the time, I lived in Chicago. I got drunk and got in an accident. The next day, I no-called, no-showed for my job. This wasn't the first time, so my employer fired me. I was low on cash and desperate, the sort of situation I'd been raised to pray for. I didn't. I filed for unemployment and while I waited for the bureaucracy to reject me, I started filling out applications. When I got hired at a couple of places that were below my standards, I turned them down and kept the search going. I was so certain that I'd find the right place, and I didn't want to settle.

A few days later, on Halloween, we had our first snowstorm. A tree branch fell on the power lines, cutting electricity to our apartment for a weekend. That first night, as the temperature rapidly fell, our home was lit by candles, beer, and laughter. One of my roommates' friends came over and, in spite of the cold, spent the night with me. I'm sure some corny line about nudity and warmth had been a catalyst, but I spent the afternoon after she'd left wondering just what the Hell was wrong with this woman. It was freezing at our place but that did nothing to slow her down. I used to pray for desire like that. What young person doesn't? Yet I didn't feel suddenly desirable; in fact, the only surprise was that she'd accepted the conditions.

I got a new job, a new routine, and new co-workers. From the outset it felt like a fun group, and I fit in quickly. Thanks to a faded encounter with one of my fellow bartenders, that fit turned into an entanglement. I walked around that place knowing I was the drama, the stir that sent us into a whirlpool of whispers and accusations. All my life I've craved and thrived in team environments, so it felt cruel to be on the outs. I wanted to leave but, knowing how difficult it is to get a service job, in Chicago, in the dead of winter, I determined that I would stay and out work everyone else, thus making myself irreplaceable.

That job did a pretty lucrative Christmas pop-up, so for

all of December every shift was packed and busy. My boss asked me to stay in town for the holiday. The trade was nine days after Christmas - including New Years - off. At the time, it was an easy choice. Even though I'd always traveled home for the holidays, what was one year off? My parents weren't ecstatic about the idea, but they acquiesced. My grandma, Yanni, agreed with my point of view, especially considering this was a new job. Christmas Eve, I spent at a co-worker's house, Christmas Day I spent with my roommates. Christmas dinner was Chinese food. Then, on the 26th, I went back to work. I didn't get home until the 29th and spent significantly less time with my family than normal. It sucked.

At the time, I had a New Year's Eve tradition of dropping acid. I don't often do psychedelics but something about the combination of powerful drugs and ringing in the new year consistently proved poignant for me. Tripping balls and freshly doused in the promise of a new beginning, I lay in bed that night pondering my lack of faith. An idea slowly unfolded, backlit by the Harlem skyline; my faith hadn't been shaken in the slightest. At every moment of doubt or difficulty throughout the past three months, from the time I vocalized my uncertainty on, I had simply turned elsewhere to find strength.

I had looked to myself.

As a child and adolescent, I'd looked to the sky for my answers. At some point, and totally by accident, I stopped doing that. What was strange was I'd done this in spite of a history of depression and anxiety, disorders that had been so bad I attempted suicide at least three times before my 21st birthday. I only say at least because when I wasn't brave enough to kill myself, I drank myself into a blackout stupor during which I may have tried a few more times, I just can't remember.

That early January 1st, 2020, I decided I didn't care where this faith in myself came from, I was just gonna act on it. I told my dad that I wanted to move to his old place in New York, but only after one more year in Chicago. That city had nurtured me, built up my faith in myself, and I wanted to honor her.

I don't need to tell you that what followed was a clusterfuck.

I won't recount here all the details of the pandemic, but personally I went from being a bartender to a distiller; I got my ass kicked at a protest outside Trump Tower; my grandmother was diagnosed with an aggressive cancer and my father's cancer began to eat away at him like a school of piranhas; I lost my job as a distiller but became a server once again; I finally stopped working in November to find myself feeling like a shark in a tank; I went home for a masked up Xmas; then nearly ruined New Year's running my mouth while rolling on Molly. Through it all I wasn't worried or afraid; I knew, somehow, I'd come out the other side of our global mess just fine, and use my strength to lift others up.

Then, 2021 happened.

In January, my grandmother died. I called her Yanni, and, in many ways, she was as much mother to me as my actual mom. Yanni took an active role in raising me. She was advocate, adversary, babysitter, chauffeur, cheerleader, chef, confidante, dance partner…shit, I could do the whole alphabet but I'm on a word count here! We didn't agree on much, but I counted on her and she emphatically delivered. As I grew up and changed, so did she. She insisted she loved me more than anyone else ever would and she proved it, time and time again.

I went home for her funeral and stayed until my bar reopened in early spring. With two and a half months left in Chicago, I fell in love. This was against all sense and better judgement, not to mention against my nature as a person. I'm a romantic, but I'm not romantic. In fact, I can be quite distant and reticent, but something about my partner and our shared views made it all too easy to fall for her. I've never tried but I imagined it'd be easier to remove and eat my arm than it was to leave her in Chicago. We wouldn't be here if I hadn't insisted we try and find something good with whatever time we had, if I hadn't felt we could be good for each other. I believe every relationship ends and when they end it sucks, no matter what. But as long as you can take something good with you, it's worth it. Every second loving her, no matter how difficult or painful the distance makes it, is worth it.

After saying goodbye to her, I worked my last shift at the bar. A handful of folks came through and then we toasted the town, drinking like fish and saying all the things that needed to be said. Back in my apartment, I had a panic attack. Why was I leaving? Didn't I love this place, these people? Hadn't I just fallen in love? In the dark and through the veil of alcohol, I tried to imagine a future away from Chicago. I couldn't. But I knew it would be an adventure, and I wanted to have that adventure! And if New York didn't work out, I could always come back.

Two days and a detour in Pittsburgh later, I was at my father's bedside. His partner had called me to tell me death was imminent, and I should come say my goodbyes. I arrived; I told him how much I loved him, how proud of him I was. He was leaving this life on his own terms. I'd always wanted to be like him, but this last act of valor solidified it; Lewis Erskine was my hero, and I would live up to his name. Then I said, "I love you, I'll see you tomorrow." He nodded, eyes closed, lips slightly apart. He didn't have the strength to say anything.

He died that night.

Friends and family offered prayer and platitudes, song, and scripture. I politely thanked them and turned my head from it all. I retreated, into my dad's old home, into the City. There were family vacations and a few solo trips, but mostly I've spent the last six months in my empty apartment, on an air mattress, doing nothing. Shattered, I look for answers, and in the dark there is only one; you can get through this. I don't know how, or how long it will take, or what my life will look like on the other side, but I know.

My mom, my last parent, likes to say, "I had a child to look into the eyes of God everyday." When I look in the mirror, I look in my eyes and see myself.

And that kid is powerful.

Francesco Garri Garripoli

God...the inside journey

God... the inside journey

The God inside... The God outside... I choose to be turned inside out... or rather, outside in... transforming the view that we have been told since childhood, that God was "outside"... or even that God was "everywhere"... how did these images to keep ME out of the mix?

...but then we are also told we can have a "direct connection" to God, still, for me, this feels like duality... it takes two 'separate' things to be involved in a connection, right? ...yet I have never felt separate from God...

Turn me inside out, and outside in... I choose surrendering to that truth we all sense in our Heart at times when we are clear, and Heart-centered, when we allow our Intuitive Mind to step up and guide us and rise beyond the bullying of our Survival and Intellectual Minds and all the programming and conditioning they've received in our life and throughout history. Our Heart Mind, that Intuitive Mind, allows us to see clearly, beyond duality at every level... Even on the God level...

Wouldn't God choose this for his children? Those in the likeness of God are pure reflections of that Infinite Consciousness Creative Grace. In my surrender, I sense immersion, as if I swim in a vast sea... Me and Sea, Me as Sea... one unified flow... An enormous school of beautiful fish all moving as one... Body, mind, spirit, God... a liquid dance of melding, like the cream in your morning coffee... swirling alchemy of light and dark that settles in harmonious brown, warm and comforting... I take it in and become that warmth, I embrace that comfort... that divine alchemy.

God in me... Me in God... this is true honor and the Creator invites us into the dance of merging, in the alchemy. We move from our "sleeping" state, driven by our conditioning and subconscious drives... There, we are like the base metals, dense and limited... In merging with God, blurring definitions of "inside" and "outside" we actually become the alchemical process in Heart Resonance… and become wide awake… Awakened once, we really can't go back to "sleep." Breathe and feel it, as words only point us to Infinity, they can't fully describe it… The God you can describe is not the Real God. So breathe again, feel Heart Resonance… not the "heart" in your chest as much as the "Heart" of the Divine… this is our birthright, what we are called to be – Awake and Free… Yes, a challenge in a world that seeks to divide and define us by our separate identities…

Breathe… trust our true and sovereign and authentic identity… This is the only truth worth expressing in every hug you share, every gaze you embrace into the eyes of another… Spirituality is a living dance that we model in all we do, say, eat, drink, and think.

Who am I? How have I allowed others to co-op my identity? Now is a good time to stop the madness… and take that deep, deep dive into the God within… I choose to become ultimately "Selfish." Embracing self as an identity beyond body, beyond mind… I re-member that I am Infinite Consciousness… God… Knowing itself through my human experience. Wow… My life is that knowing. My life is that revealing. My life is that remembering. Unique I am as "my human experience" is absolutely unique and Infinite Consciousness expresses through me – knows itself through me – in a way that it cannot through any other human. No one does me better than me, so I am asked to own it, embrace it, embrace the Love of the Divine. I stop and breathe into that… I pause and ponder and wonder how I can question my worth, my value. If Infinite Consciousness God is knowing itself through me, expressing itself through me, well, my uniqueness is critical for that expression.

No one can do me better than me. No matter how I may judge myself… how I may wish for some different version of me, richer version of me, smarter version of me, prettier version of me, I am exactly the perfect expression of Infinite Consciousness God, playing it out through me, precisely how I am in this moment. Breathe into that… Accept that. The God in Me expresses exactly in the form and style I am.

Now, it's time to own that. Now, it's time to honor that. Now, it's time to celebrate that.

Dancing through me is pure life-force… in the tradition of Qigong from China that I practice and teach, this "life-force" is called Qi (chee). If I were Zulu, I would use the word Umoya, Greeks called it Pneuma, West African culture call it Ase… but no matter what the name, it is the Divine source of life. How willing are we to honor that energy dancing through every cell, every atom inside our body? How willing are we to be grateful for this expression of the divine in every breath we take?

Life is a dance of remembering and forgetting… of being at peace and then tumbling into chaos. This life may be precisely defined to be like this, and in this dance, we are asked to show our stuff… to stand up to the mirror of the Universe, the mirror of everyone we meet, the mirror of every situation we face, and ask, "Am I ready to accept the truth of who I am?" Maybe this life is not meant to be smooth all the time, and that our desire for that "perfection" only sets us up for failure. Then, when we fail, we judge ourselves – or worse, point blame to others. Like Miles Davis once said, "It's not the wrong note you play, it's the note you play right after that note that really matters."

We are on this most curious journey… and yes, there are lots of wrong notes being played all the time it seems… but when I can take that step back and take a deep breath, I can remember to see it all through the window of my Heart Resonance. This is when I return to my remembering… This is when I sense that I truly am Infinite Consciousness God Essence expressing through me, knowing itself through my very human experience. In that remembering I am free, I am sovereign, I am responsible for taking my next breath… and in that breath, allowing myself to model and radiate the God that shines through all I say and do and feel and pray…

…and what is "community" except recognizing that the "God inside" is also "inside" each and every person – whether they can see it or not. We are brought together with other souls not because we always agree on everything, but many times, we are there to stay in our Heart Resonance even when we don't agree… Guided by Heart, we allow the multiplicity of views, multiplicity of expressions of that "God inside" and in that way, we all come together in recognition of this truth. From there, we are simply asked to be free, and model that freedom knowing that we are inextricably woven together with every other soul in our community. What else can weave this magical tapestry of humanity?

The God inside is the great weaver... I surrender into this beautiful and creative dance... Will you join me?

Archie Ivy

The God Within

The God Within

When dealing with any kind of a concept of God - the basic notion there – is that concept is based on an individual definition or understanding because, as scientists would say, there is a lack of supporting concrete evidence of the very existence of a God. One's journey with God starts with a believe that God is.

And so I categorize them in two areas, God, with a capital G, and god with a small G. God with a small G is a number of things, or I should say would be anything that a person puts a high priority upon to the level of worship. With some people, that could be habits. Some people, it could be material things, some people, it can be other people if they have that kind of a dominance, a dominant person in their reality. But as far as the capital G God, the greater God, in my opinion, that notion is again an individual thing. And it's about how one's concept of that God is. Personally, I do not take to the notion of an ageless yet old white-haired guy sitting on a throne that uses his hands to manipulate events in a world over which he governs. That belief appears to be held by many if not most of those who believe in God.

However, I believe that that particular image of God is from a standpoint of us thinking of God based on how we are, making him in our image, as opposed to us being made in his image. I am a Christian by faith, meaning that I follow a theology based on the teachings of Christ. I do understand that there are others, but I personally believe that there is one God, and that God is a unifying force that connects all things. The greatest force. The force of creation. How can I describe it? It is a being, a "consciousness" that exists on a higher plane than what we - as humans - are on or can even imagine. We exist in a physical realm measured in three dimensions. In biblical scripture, it states clearly that God is a spirit. I perceive that spirit joins, is part of, all things that exist in and throughout the universe, all matter and all non-matter. I'm reluctant to describe that energy as intelligence because it is an intelligence higher than what we imagine intelligence to be. But it's a unified force that holds it altogether and is a commonality in and to all things.

To me it was that intelligence that formed the energy that caused creation, what Science likes to call the Big Bang. It is the same intelligence which keeps a wonderful balance between chaos and a unified orchestration of synchronicity of existence, the wonder to the heavens. The planets exist at a definite spacing between one another. And still they feed off each other's energy. And I think that that type of orchestration goes beyond what our ability to see in telescopes or imagine but is what I would consider to be the God force. That being said, the God in me, the accessing of that God force, is how we connect to that spirit. In the biblical tradition, they speak of God as being a Trinity figure, one God in three persons. You have God the father who is the creator, God the son who walked among us in human form as savior the of humanity, and then God the spirit, which is our connection to him in the day-to-day basis, and we receive his spirit just by asking. My journey has brought me to this destination…

Diem Jones

The Journey
STILL
Air in the New Year
Look In
Neo-Landings: Techno Primal Questions
The Dog in Me
...and so it IS

The Journey

Is God a minion of we the peoples, who so unabashedly and shamelessly take for granted that another day will come. Hmmmm

God is…what?
God is…where?
God is…why?

What
…and so it seems to me that an unadulterated God might be vaporous, or nebulously adrift. For me, God is the interconnection between soul, skin, and spirit, thus my definition of God is an unblemished rhythm that we each have been gifted to save us from ourselves.

Where
…and so it seems to me that God is an unalloyed shapeshifter around and within each of us. There is no place that God does not influence, guide, or affect. Gifted with an omnidirectional, two-way looking glass, making the eye of God spatially omnipresent.

Why
…and so it seems to me, we have a bi-directional need to balance soul, skin and spirit, and a connection with the place or being we call God, is not always clear-cut, albeit necessary to better understand self —a primal and primary instinct.

STILL

Be STILL and….
Know
Listen
Move
…answer the call

Standing Tall in the Light of Love

Call the answers…
Move
Listen
Know
…to be Still and flowing into your inner self

Be STILL and….
Know
Listen
Move
…answer the call

Love the Light and Stand Tall
…stand for something or Fall.

Air in the New Year

The air which we breathe could always kill us…we are just more aware of it now!

This is not an expose on the impacts of the current pandemic, but rather a comment on the arrival of new consciousness amongst a growing wave of our global societies. Yes this is an acknowledge of awakenings, which I have come to embrace as necessary steps in our evolution, since we have been on a cycle of devolution for eons.

In the beginning there was one, which split into two, which split into four, which split into sixteen and so on. The ONE is a concept I think shines light on the roots of our origins and the relationship and relativity we have with each other.

Sadly, it is the uncovering of these and other truths that have sparked fear, jealously, hatred and balls of confusion. Story tellers have created many tales to calm this storm, as evidenced by the fabled tale of the McCoys and the Hatfields, and many others. It is the root of these misplaced-egoisms that have been the center of wars, genocides, tribal upheavals, conquering and other forms of domination. Seems sad to me that relatives would choose waring with one another over peace…. also, economics do seem to also sprinkle through these tribulations as wars are often based on the control of monetizable resources.

They who control the resources, can come to control or direct the mindset of the recipients. Is global domination a science-fiction screenplay or a reality we see being played out by world leaders?

The air which we breathe could always kill us…we are just more aware of it now!

We have an opportunity to course correct and so it seems that if we don't align ourselves with this mindset, we will destroy the planet we call home before we have cultivated another one to move to….

...Mother Earth has landed for the third time and we all have knocked her up. We have taken from the teachings of the pyramids and twisted the truth to suit our needs, but in the end.... truth is in the light.

My prayer for us [beginning with me] is to self reflect and decide what are the consequences of our projections.

Think before you walk
Think before you talk
Think before you move
Decide which way you choose to grove....

Follow your follow,
But know thyself so you know best which direction is up...

I look up when I pray
Each and every day,
As I look into the mirror to take a deeper dive.

¿r.u. Cyrius?

Look In...

*Looking in a looking glass...Looking through a looking glass...looking
without a looking glass
and finding the mirror is your new best friend.*

Sometimes it seems that people are not open for what another is
hoping for. So, the hoper, better now known as the HopeE, gets
very, very frustrated because there's no reception. But Hope-Ees
must remember that it is their desire or ego placement that often
drive what it is we choose to share, and when to share it. The
return? How can you push something out, expect a return and then
get disappointed? Put it out there if you feel it's right. Let it flow,
and then you'll know.

...get down on the good foot and up on the new-found wing.

I think we need to mind what we do and be careful who we share
what we do with, because not all of our do is is everybody...Some
things aren't receivable, because people have a do limit...if they're
not even managing their own do, how do you think they can handle
your do? That's just too much to do-do for one person to handle.
And you know what happens when you overload with do-do?
You shut down. That's when the pipes break, that's when you call
Roto-Rooter, but that's expensive. That is not the path to wellness.
So, mind your do, because there's someone out there who woke up
knowing your do is not for them.

Get down on the good foot and up on the new-found wing...

... here some of us are in the dawn of the 22nd century trying to
manage our primal instincts.

Done yet, or still brewing your do?

¿r.u. with US?
¿r.u. with THEM?
¿r.u. with U?

The looking glass knows what the shadow does not…Look first at your reflection before you gaze at your projections.

Neo Landings: Techno-Primal Questions

Do NOT attempt to adjust your reality
The I.T. has landed and decided to wrangle control
Do NOT attempt to find your old reality
The I.T. has landed and decided the new in you:

The WHO
The WHAT
The WHERE
The WHEN and
…. then The WHY

Since the beginning of recorded time, the strongest, most durable, longest lasting building material has been built on the backs of my ancestors, and since we are all related at the root core — my ancestors are related to your ancestors, which makes what's mine could be yours and what's yours could be mine, in part….another part of the equation is that we have been guided to stay on the surface and not to look within…not to look deeper…NOT to look into the looking glass, as there as been a conspiracy to keep you and I from kissing the mirror!

Zeroes and Ones are my heroes, making the she's and he's sometimes she-roes and just like Michael, it's time for us ALL to row the boat ashore. It's time to rebuild after the battles of Jherico and Jheri-curls…It's time to build forward after learning that yesterday's tomorrow came with tears of shame, while fanning the flames of the desired programming. They almost won, BUT the Zeroes and Ones were misread.

Misreading is the disbelief in yourself, thus the power of the misread was a desired outcome of the dominant cultures of misthinkers. They became greedy stinkers, who had mastered the era of "The Delusion of Confusion" aka the D.C.

It was in the DC or the DMV that the fears of whites became the fuel of hatred, but after much numbing and dumbing down…

hmmm—so and show is right! We've been shown that since we all share some inner matters of DNA and RNA and we are more alike than different…IN FACT, we all are related. Why should this be so frightening?

…if my ancestors and your ancestors we distant cousins, how could we be unrelated…when then did we fall for the programming, of the Zeroes and Ones? Did it start in the 1940's with the advent of DAT [digital audio tape]? Did it start with the discovery of neurons and protons? Did it start with the invention of gunpowder or bronze? Did it start when my people had year-round gardens and yours learned to store and protect food? When did mine or yours become bigger and better?

I think there is a master plan and we wrote the script. While many would want you to think that they are the masters and in control, their plan is flawed as it is built on lies, deceit, deception and greed.

Every drip is the precursor of a drop and since we come from the original "drips" our drops of blood are related. We all then, according to the Jim Crow Laws, are negroid. Why should this be so frightening and viewed as a threat to some who are guided by a misaligned ego-construct that harps on a pho-reality of skin tones being divisive lines of disembarkation syndrome.

How can we be anything else but friends¿

Do NOT attempt to adjust your reality
The I.T. has landed and decided to wrangle control
Do NOT attempt to find your old reality
The I.T. has landed and decided the new in you:

The WHO
The WHAT
The WHERE
The WHEN and
…. then The WHY

¿r.u. Cyrius?

The Dog in Me

Feet are for landings…wings don't fail me now!

I recall many things in the course of my lifetime while remaining
in deepest appreciation and gratitude for the opportunity to receive
as well as share the depths of my breath…I am still here and pinch
myself regularly…wowWOW-meow, as the dog in me emanates
from the God in me.

If my prayers remain stationary, it can be a dogma that leads me, so
I have come to move my feet when I pray…I allow my feet, soul,
bones and heart to also look up when I pray, as it is this direction I
claim a path to my destiny.

While I believe there is both a heaven and a hell, I also find a
miracle in the oceans between them. If hell is below, we've all
been there or at least have had a taste, which for some, a desired
succulence is found…which is different than my view. My views
my be different than your views and all can be-in peace.

I stand, you walk…I frown, you smile…I rise, you find a seat
and all on the same planet…it is on the same earth we have been
graced with living our respective and chosen walks…it is on this
rock I rest to hear your words—observe your actions and compare
that with your speak. Judgmental comparisons do not serve me, but
rather the lessons learned from the observations.

I move my feet when I pray
I look up when I pray
I choose to lift myself up vs
Beating my self down…
…peace can stand still
And I will clutch and embrace it under my wing.

Glory hollers and is not stupid.

...and so it IS

In the aftermath of the undertow and the overflow we can now decide what it is that we desire to fill our cups....

Our cups have overflowed with indecision, discontent, radial eyes and lies to bring us to the crossroads...

My choice, your choice, and the choices of the alabaster baked cookies:
- Is it love that you are running from or is hatred your end game?
- Are the teachings of our ancestors to be heeded or re-sewn?
- Is your hiding place amongst the unbridled sheep that silently wish a wash?
- Are the pops on the top of your sickle for slicing or dicing?
- Can we get the long and windy pathways to straighten up?
- Can we learn to hear the received meanings of our words?

In the aftermath of the undertow and the overflow we can now decide what it is that we desire to fill our cups....

Are we to:
> love to love,
>> love to hate,
>>> hate to love,
>>>> hate in the name of love....
>>>>> or bring in new noise...

The pleasures of exhaustion are the fruits of our labor and our chariots are destined to roar.... I pray for a destination that embraces us all before we fall...

Falling from the edge of the precipice of no-return is not where I choose to be...I've learned to kiss my mirror and from there, I know blossoms of light will adorn me and all of us who dare to allow love to be at the center and at the end of the road.

...and so it is and can be!

¿r.u. Cyrius?

O.N.E. [One Never Escapes]

Marc A. Kline

Blaspheme the Meme

Blaspheme the Meme?

Jacob woke from his dream and exclaimed, "God was in this place, and I, I did not know it." Awakening in the hills of Beth El, Jacob met God. We give this story a great deal of attention as one of the most impactful epiphanic stories in the Bible. But, if we are diligent, we read the rest of the story. The best we can say is that Jacob becomes aware that something is out there. No one can read the text and argue that he is, as yet a believer. "If God will be with me and will watch over me on this journey I am taking and will give me food to eat and clothes to wear so that I return safely to my father's household, then Adonai will be my God." (Gen 28:21-22)

I would argue that most people's relationship with "God" lies somewhere close to this. We believe in the moments of proof, cast aside the relationship when we don't get our way, but most of the time, live ambivalently tangent to anything or any notion divine. Then, we sit and wonder why life lacks meaning and direction.

I have no idea what God is. In fact, my tradition argues that defining God is blasphemy. How can one with human-limitations even think about making God tangible and limited? Perhaps the greatest problem we face in the world is that we have become too tangible. We have forgotten how to dream. The horizons of our eyesight have become the boundaries of our faith. "The God within" becomes the God who does or ignores our bidding, who accepts my version while rejecting everyone else. Even while our world experience cannot comport with this myopic notion of divinity, we find in religious voices, the seeds growing fear and anxiety. Simply, we are shackled by our inability to leap and dream with faith. If one asks us, "Where is God?" our default answer falls somewhere between, "There is no God" and, "Only where I want God to be."

People speak of having a "fear" of God. Some who worship do so out of the fear of repercussions for not worshipping. Some who reject God do so believing that this type of God couldn't make sense. In Hebrew, the word "

I have no idea what God is. God has never tapped my shoulder and told me how the Source of Creation feels about potato salad, corned beef, professional athletics, or world politics. I absolutely believe, though, that there is a force much greater than anything I can fathom that controls/coordinates more than I could ever understand.

A friend of mine, Dr. Rev Daisy Machado, served as the President of the Lexington Theological Seminary. At her installation, she spoke the most prophetic words. She admonished us to stop trying to prove that God exists or what God is. She told us that the real work of faith is to demonstrate what God does to help fix the world.

My God does. The call from the source of Salvation to which I respond tells me that heaven and earth cannot ever touch if I am not reaching beyond the "me" to help lift and empower the "we." I have no salvation reserved for just me. In the same sense that justice can never be "just us," the world cannot be whole while some of us flourish on the backs of, or in ignorance of another. I also understand that God cannot do what I refuse to do. If I don't help feed the hungry, they will starve. If I don't help lift the fallen, they will languish and fade. If I don't help teach and learn; grow and evolve, we will falter into chaos.

JD (John D.) Parran

The God Within

The God Within

The God within me has always been real... compared to God, the Fatherwho art in Heaven.... the Creator.....the Almighty....Jehovah.......Allah.......Yahweh...El Shaddai.... Al-Muhaimin.......

The Christian teachings were usually about how to help one become holy or simply righteous. Like the Charles Mingus composition, "Better Git Hit In Your Soul."

So-ul!!.... Soul. Oh yeah, we got plenty of that.... don't we?

Baptism, however, was to be "born again" into a higher level of bliss and responsibility. You are supposed to really have God in you now.

Who am I to have God within me?

I have always doubted my belief in this ultimate (intimate?) entity. Raised in faith, to "believe", I am still caught up in my everyday quests for the survival of me in the world. What does THAT have to do with the Within? At a young age I gradually started to conceptualize God as me, probably on account of the Protestant responsibility laid on in sermons and Sunday School: "Nothing stands between you and your Maker."

Well, you are taught to pray as a baby. The first memorization exercises are the Lord's Prayer and the 23rd Psalm. "On your knees, please. Talk to Him. Ask him to make you a good boy." Maybe for my parents, I was God there in prayer, in fulfilment of their family values and needs. Me, "...thine is the Kingdom, Power and Glory, forever (and bless Mommy and Daddy, let the angels watch over them, Amen." Here at least there was the suggestion that I was fortunate to have parents, living together with them in a calm, secure home. I knew that that was a blessing because not everybody in the Hood had it.

Thank God. Right!

Now my mother, she had the Faith. Other folk danced, cried and "got happy" in Jesus' name all around Christ Southern Mission

Baptist Church…nothing exceptional there… but when Mama got "happy" then I could actually feel it. It frightened me because of the disconnect to her in a way I didn't know I was connected. This was her love for me on which she always focused and I didn't have to know about it. When that well ran dry as the "Spirit" entered her and burst out of her voice… "Hallelujah, praise Jesus" … for just a few minutes I felt the difference, vividly. She kept me next to her in the Mothers Board pew until the church moved location for urban renewal about the time of my puberty. So, I was physically touching her when the spirit hit that Sunday before when she uttered those exaltations, rose up and pranced down the aisle to the coat room/nurses station to compose herself before coming back to me. What a relief, the spirit was gone. My mother came back to me. Was God then gone?

My dad, J D Sr., articulated the global formula for adulthood to me. I was about 10 or 11 years old, and he probably said it more than once. At the time I was not able to perceive concepts globally even if I think I do now. He said, "When you reach 13 years of age God holds you responsible." Responsible for what? I thought I knew the answer. The Commandments pretty much covered it. I was aware or right/wrong, good/bad…but no. My inner response to myself was simply, "Oh, no worries then. I'll never reach 13." Not that I would die young but that the 2 or 4 years in the future were incomprehensible in terms of days, weeks, months, years. Maybe this is the manifestation of the God within who moves time so quickly through summer vacation from school but the future immediately after vacation seems endless before you.

Like my understanding of God, Time moves in mysterious ways. I don't always know what I am doing in my creative professional life or in creating my life overall. Does God know?

Along with cultural religious behavior we must decide how to treat others…."as you would treat yourself." A simple axiom on the surface presuming you are good to yourself. The God within has to make this choice, as usual. Do you treat others as you want to be treated or do you treat them the way They want? Your very survival can depend on how you handle situations involving others. The God within must help you maneuver when society around you doesn't allow free choice to do as You believe. Power and governance work either for the community or against enemies (or both simultaneously) not intending to please anyone. They appear to act on the instructions of God, inner or from "above" in order solve the dilemma at hand. Let's think about how we deal with the dichotomies of choice when we're up against walls of fear and doubt about the simple choices that clash with morality or just don't jive the comfort level of how we respond to or present (the verb) attitude in dealing with all the "Thems."

So, there is an inner battle going on. Is God even part of the argument? I am grateful that my planetary goals align with my values much of the time. When they don't match-up I usually have a reason. (Or is that reason just a temptation to violate my own morality?)

Through my adaptation of new/older African and Original American belief systems I can finally connect Heaven and Hell or… in the best sense I have permission to collapse those concepts of split spirituality. Here I leverage myself like and unlike the Prodigal Son…. I find my own way back… to my own Home.

Carol A. Penn

The God Within

The God Within

I am Carol, daughter of Alma, daughter of Marion, daughter of Marion, daughter of Phoebe, daughter of women whose names I cannot know but whose dreams are in the story of my bones.

I am Carol, daughter of William Arthur, son of William Robert, son of a man whose name I do not know who is the son of men I cannot know but whose dreams are in the story of my bones.

It is there in the story of my bones that perhaps I can find God again, for you see the God that was for so long never further away than my fingertips, seems to have moved somewhere, no longer quite so accessible, no longer so easily reached or felt at the end of my fingertips.

I have been examining this phenomenon lately, this shift in where God is, my sense and understanding of God, of all that is greater than myself has always been a felt sense, a physical knowing, an understanding that this relationship is most tenderly revealed in relationship to others. A lifelong, committed, hopeful optimist, God has never been any further than my next breath, my next heartbeat.

In recent years my certainty has regarding knowing God has shifted just as my certainty of the location of God within has shifted. I have been trying to pinpoint the origin story of this shift and it is becoming clear to me that God began to change addresses internally when the political campaign of 2015 left behind a culture of thoughtlessness, confusion, hatred, and displacement along with a growing sensation that there was a lessening sense of belonging for me, my husband, my sons, my immediate and extended family.

As time passed the vile just kept becoming more vile, the hate closer and closer to the surface, more freely spoken, more blatant as racially motivated assaults and murders continued to grow. Blossoming in the most surprising of places, like the mushrooms that sprang up on my mother's lawn every summer, unbidden, unwelcome, surprising. All the while God was shifting inside of me to places initially familiar but soon to places less familiar and God began to feel the way muscles seldom used would feel when you work out after not moving for a long time. I began to hurt and ache in places where I did not know I could hurt and ache. I knew God was finding a new address inside of me moving away from the familiar, seeking new places in me, just as I was seeking new places in the recesses of my mind to protect myself from the ongoing onslaught of lies and 'alternate truths' that I was supposed to believe as real.

2016 ushered in an error of rudeness and hate in this country and a parade of senseless murders, hate crimes, gun violence, intimate partner violence that made even the most pious ask, God where are you and why are you allowing these things, such suffering, such despair? I continued to notice that the God within me, that was always so close to the surface, on my sleeve, on the tip of my tongue was steadily retreating from the front lines of my body. The God that had always been so easily accessible to me, seemed to be saying enough.

2017, 2018 children murdering other children, guns more guns, the God in me wanted to speak and so wrote a book, Meditation in a Time of Madness. Perhaps God was in my brain, my fingertips, perhaps the God in me was best now expressed as a storyteller, at least for now at least for this moment.

2019 a woman, a relative that I often loved more than life itself passed from this life, in February of 2020, my brother, and a beloved uncle flew away from Earth school, taking more pieces of God with them, the pieces of God that were still near enough to the surface of my skin, these pieces flew out of me as if they were flint drawn to a magnet.

2020 more meditation in a time of madness, friends leaving Earth school, unexpected and unexplained illness and the devil itself, in the form of an invisible virus. Those close to me, my mother, my child's father, threatened by illness other than the pandemic, no way out, only deeper pathways in and where now is God?

Focused on safety, focused on keeping my mother out of the clutches of the devil, my world becomes shrink wrapped and God sits outside of me, on the edge of the bed. God now comes in and out because God has mostly relocated to my throat, coming through deep sighs and sobs that escape my throat on a more and more frequent basis. God is the lump in my throat, God is my breaking heart. It is the first time in my life where I realize that God does not always show up as a happy feeling or a soothing feeling. I am learning that God comes in shades of sadness and sorrow, doubt, uncertainty, pain especially when all of the discomfort is born out of love and longing for life.

2021 the inevitable, death comes, my mother in my arms, God in my auditory canal as the whispering of her dying breath filled my ears, like a song being sung by some strange exotic other worldly bird. God dies, a mother dies, a woman is fully born in me, through me, as me.

Where now could God therefore be, floating in the air all around me, floating on her last breath, I inhale and God renters me as the sensation of my mothers last breath, entering my nostrils, being warmed in my sinus passages, making its way down my trachea into the bronchioles, branching into my lungs, filling the alveoli, into the base of each lung where the rich capillary beds will carry God deep into the rest of me. God making her way back, back to mother mitochondria, back to the marrow of my bones, the marrow that links me to the long and weary dreams of my mothers and fathers whose names I cannot know but here in the marrow of my own bones, I meet them, I meet her, and I discover God within once more.

Amy Shimsohn-Santo

I Am Turning a Key

I Am Turning a Key

opening windows & doors
removing the roof, dismembering
my sensibilities & assumptions
about what is possible
yesterday is not a boarded box
sent from south to north
or east to west
in search of freedom
after a series of deaths,
what does your life still say to you?
what does it want?
everything —including now,
was made by something
that did not know it was possible

Toussaint L

God is my ALL: The God in Me

God is my ALL. The God in Me.

God is my all. All things are possible.

My roots are grounded in the Christian faith. My family heritage came out of the brutality of slavery, reconstruction, and Jim Crow apartheid against my Black people. Yet, like the Jews in the Bible, my family held on to faith that the Lord would bring us out. My grandmother had enormous faith, studied, and trained to become a pastor of a church. It was not to be because she could not be a pastor in certain denominations as a woman. My grandmother was an Evangelist. My Grandmother and Grandfather taught their children, our parents, about the power of prayer. In turn, our parents took us to church, led us to pray, and showed us how "prayer changes things."

As a child in Sunday School, I learned Bible Stories. As an adult reading the Bible, I see how faith in the Lord and worship resulted in miracles, survival, winning against impossible odds, overcoming illness, poverty, hunger, and death through prayer and faith. The many Bible stories continue to inspire and intrigue me: Noah, Jonah in the Whale, Daniel in the lion's den, three men in a fiery furnace, Jesus raising Lazarus from the dead, and Jesus overcoming his death on the cross and his resurrection.

I begin and end my days with prayer. As I arise and walk, I get on my knees, and I thank God for the many blessings of life, good health, family, spiritual and financial prosperity. I thank God for another day filled with hope, opportunities, and possibilities. I pray for my family, our nation, our world, and for peace. I believe prayer changes things.

I find great comfort and hope in Bible verses that resonate with me and are in my heart.

Romans 8:28 "And we know all things work together for good to them who love God and who are called according to his purpose."

Mark 9:23 "If thou canst believe, all things are possible to him that believeth."

Phillipians 4:3 "I can do all things through Christ who strengthens me."

I live my life mission through Luke 12:48, "Too whom much is given, much will be required." I believe the opportunities I have received are to be shared. I am mightily blessed in my life with education, training, and opportunity. At every turn where I learned a skill, mastered a talent, or entered a space, I left the door open, and I reached back and lifted up. I see my life as a channel, a ladder, and an open window. I know that education and opportunity can change things, so I devote my life to giving back. I believe "Service is the rent we pay for the privilege of living on this earth." If we have been blessed with talents, wealth, knowledge, time, and the like, I believe we are required to help others. My faith and work are prayers in action.

My mind has a continual conversation with me. Sometimes, my mind wanders to fear, viewing life and challenges expecting the worst, visualizing failure. In my faith, I have learned that to counter these negative thoughts, I must counteract them with positive thoughts and affirmations. Being mindful and intentional about my ideas helps me move with imagination, courage, and energy.

The hymn captures my sentiments "Our thoughts are prayers. And we are always praying. Our thoughts are prayers. Listen to what you are saying. Take charge of what you are saying."

I call on affirmations to lift myself, to put on armor as I face life's many trials, challenges, and opportunities. I pray for the outcomes, experience, and results I want in my day. I was taught when you pray, you give it to God and wait for an answer. I am impatient. I find it hard to just "wait." I am of the mind that the Lord helps those who help themselves, so I push, pull, and continue to pray while working to bring about a result.

I pray. When the answer comes, it may be: Yes, No, Not yet, Not this, but something better than you can imagine and beyond what you asked is what I have for you. My father had an expression, "Another prayer answered." The phrase is ambiguous. I claim this expression for myself. I love to proclaim, "Another prayer answered, Yes when the Lord has healed someone.

Living with faith lifts my soul, raises my consciousness, and elevates everything I do. I call on the ALL to help me do all things.

I have learned that with faith in God, ALL things work together for good. I recognize there are many faiths, and many call the Creator by different names and have many ways to show devotion. I celebrate all the many who believe in a higher power. I acknowledge and accept that all are not believers, and I respect their rights.

I do not think one religion or faith is over another. Rather, the key is to respect all. The Eleventh Commandment in the New Testament is simple: "Love one another."

Mona R. Washington

My Jesus Drinks Malbec

My Jesus Drinks Malbec

Characters: Kim   36, Barry's wife
                  Barry   38, Kim's husband
                  Laura   36, Kim's high school friend
                  Cell Group Attendees of various ages and
backgrounds, no fewer than 3

Setting: A Philadelphia suburb. Kim and Barry's basement in their home.

Time: Early evening. The 2,022nd year of our Lord and Savior: Jesus the Christ.

Across a small table, which holds a cross and a hymnal, CELL GROUP ATTENDEES sit and face KIM and BARRY, who stand. LAURA rushes down the basement stairs.

KIM: I'm so happy I ran into you at the market this morning.
LAURA: Me too.
KIM: What a nice surprise.
LAURA: It sure was. Maybe moving back here won't be so bad.
KIM: Well, I'm glad you could make it.
LAURA: Sorry I'm late.
KIM: You're fine. We've already made our introductions, but you can catch up when we have our potluck afterward.

KIM gestures for LAURA to take a seat.

KIM (CONT'D): Everyone, I'd like you to welcome Laura. We've been friends since high school.
CELL GROUP ATTENDEES: Hi Laura…. Hello…Welcome.

LAURA smiles and sits in the front row.

BARRY: We welcome you in the spirit of Christian Unity and

Peace.

KIM: That's my husband, Barry.

LAURA: Hi.

BARRY: Let us bow our heads for intercessory prayer.

Heads bow.

BARRY (CONT'D): Heavenly Father, we ask that you bless us with the Holy Spirit and lead us in the true Christian way. Deliver us from false prophets and false religions. Lord, we have those among us who're searching for a release, to be delivered from Jehovah's Witnesses and Mormons. They are--

LAURA: Excuse me?

Everyone stares at LAURA.

KIM: Laura?

LAURA: What was that you said about deliverance?

BARRY: We're asking for protection from false prophets.

KIM: Are you a Jehovah's Witness?

LAURA: That's not the point. I'd prefer to pray for understanding, not against any particular religion.

Several CELL GROUP ATTENDEES nod in affirmation.

KIM: We weren't trying to offend anyone.

LAURA: I'd rather err on the side of inclusion, not exclusion.

BARRY coughs loudly. He bows his head, and everyone follows suit.

BARRY: Thank you for your comments, Laura…Dear Father God, keep us safe from all sin and depravity. Help us all to be comfortable with the course you have set for us.

LAURA: That's not germane.

KIM: Really.

LAURA: Really. It's not even Michael, Marlon, Tito, or Jackie.

Some CELL GROUP ATTENDEES laugh.

BARRY: What?

LAURA: I don't think God is hung up on depravity, maybe sin but…you know, I also don't know if we should pray for comfort.

KIM: Why not?

CELL GROUP ATTENDEE: What's wrong with comfort?

LAURA: Nothing. I think God's busy and being comfortable shouldn't necessarily be a priority. You know Jesus was Out There. He wore a dress, but were his sandals comfortable? We have to accept Jesus as he was---

BARRY: What are you implying about his sexual orientation?

KIM: Ha! I just got it.

LAURA: Jesus' sexual orientation?

KIM: No. The Jackson Five joke.

BARRY: Kim!

KIM shrugs, then sits with the rest of the CELL GROUP ATTENDEES.

BARRY: Laura, I have to draw a line.

LAURA: Sure you do. But is your line everyone else's?

BARRY: You're telling me you think Jesus was gay?

LAURA: Maybe. Yes. No. Who knows? He could have been bisexual, heterosexual, pansexual--

BARRY: My God, Laura.

LAURA: That's just the point.

CELL GROUP ATTENDEE: This is better than intercessory prayer.

LAURA: Barry, don't blaspheme. You need to think about what you're saying.

What if Jesus was gay?

All stare at her for an Eternity.

LAURA (CONT'D): Would that change the meaning of the Gospels for you? Would it undermine your view of Christianity?

BARRY: I've never read anything that says Jesus was gay. Have you?

LAURA: I've never read anything that says he's not gay.

CELL GROUP ATTENDEE: Hmm. Neither have I.

BARRY: You're making this up.

LAURA: No, I'm not. Think about it: Jesus the Christ--
KIM: 'the Christ'?
LAURA: Yes. Jesus the Christ wore a dress, drank wine constantly, and hung around twelve men. Gay cabaret?
KIM: Oh Laura. You're being ridiculous.
LAURA: What about Mary Magdalene?
BARRY: Dare I ask, what about her?
LAURA: She wasn't really that deep into his posse.
KIM: His posse?
BARRY: Kim! Don't engage her.
LAURA: Yeah Kim. Don't engage me. But can you marry me?
CELL GROUP ATTENDEE: I thought the point was that we can all do everything. Sure. I could marry you.
BARRY: Why would you think that?
LAURA: My goodness. I don't. I don't know anyone well enough to marry them. We just met. Except for Kim. I guess I could marry her.

Some CELL GROUP ATTENDEES snicker.

BARRY: What are you--
LAURA: You know Barry, I was thinking. Mary Magdalene wasn't following him around all the time. But she was there when it counted. You know how we do.
KIM: Who?
LAURA: Women.
CELL GROUP ATTENDEE: I thought Mary Magdalene was with him the whole time.
LAURA: Post-demons, supposedly. Maybe. But that's why I'm reading the Gospel of Mary. I like how she stood up to Peter. I don't like him so much.
KIM: Where did you get that book?
LAURA: Where did you get your Bible?
CELL GROUP ATTENDEE: This is a little more 'Bible study' than I thought it'd be.

One CELL GROUP ATTENDEE exits.

LAURA: It's not like those white guys in Europe were thinking about us…or anyone besides themselves. I think you have to at least question that big conference. It wasn't like they were conferring with Essence or Ms. Magazine.

CELL GROUP ATTENDEE: I don't think we should get racial.

BARRY: You can't just play fast and loose with the Bible, Laura.

LAURA: I'm not. The Gnostic Gospels are so liberating. You know. Free your Spirit…look inward for the Divine, not outside of yourself.

CELL GROUP ATTENDEE: That sounds like an Eastern religion.

LAURA: That's a bad thing? Works for me.

BARRY: Let's stick to the Bible.

LAURA: Which one?

CELL GROUP ATTENDEE: Which one?

LAURA: And which translation? Are you including the apocrypha?

CELL GROUP ATTENDEE: She has a point. My uncle is Catholic and his Bible has more books.

BARRY: I'm talking about the Bible right here on this devotion table.

LAURA: Why do you think that's the right Bible?

BARRY: I suppose you know what the 'right' Bible is?

LAURA: I'm just saying. What about the gap?

KIM: The gap? OK. OK. I get it this time. Jesus wore jeans from the Gap.

LAURA: Maybe. They'd seem hot. I always thought of Jesus as practical, with maybe a toolkit under his dress.

BARRY: He was not wearing a dress.

CELL GROUP ATTENDEE: Well, Barry. You weren't there.

LAURA: OK. Let's say he wasn't wearing a dress. What about that gap? Bar mitzvah, and then the Big Curtain. What was he doing all of those years?

CELL GROUP ATTENDEE: Yeah, what was he doing?

LAURA: I hope he was having fun.

BARRY: Laura. Please stop. This is Bible study.

LAURA: Precisely. That's why we should be reading The Quran.

BARRY: We're not here to study the Quran.

LAURA: The Quran mentions Jesus more times than any Bible I know about.

I think it's always interesting that folks want to stick to one sacred text.

KIM: It's not a 'sacred text.'

LAURA: It's not?

KIM: It is. You know what I mean. It's the Bible.

BARRY: What would you have us add? There's a Biblical prohibition on false books.

LAURA: Show me where it says there can't be more sacred texts. Look at the Book of Mormon.

BARRY: We're not here to study the Book of Mormon.

CELL GROUP ATTENDEE: Why not?

LAURA: Look, as literature, it's the only truly American theology. You know--

BARRY: Let's take a 5-minute break.

LAURA begins to exit.

KIM: You're leaving?

LAURA: I'll be right back. I'm just getting my contribution for the potluck.

KIM: OK.

LAURA: Do you have glasses?

BARRY: Sure. Why?

LAURA: It's a bottle of Malbec.

KIM: Malbec?

LAURA: You know, a red wine everyone can enjoy and afford. I always think of Jesus as drinking something 'fruity'---

BARRY: Please stop.

LAURA: 'Fruity' and smooth--like a Malbec. Thick-skinned grapes and all----right? My Jesus is more of a Malbec savior than a Riesling one. I'll be right back.

LAURA exits.

BARRY: She's not coming to the next Cell Group meeting.

THE END-ISH

Kerwin Webb

The Essential Journey – The Journey to Me

The Essential Journey – The Journey to Me

Have you ever felt like you were created to do a certain thing, and then life got in the way? This is exactly what I felt from the time I was around twelve through the years of young adulthood. I had this overwhelming feeling of inadequacy, and felt that I was ill-suited for many of the tasks that I engaged in. A good student who excelled academically, I was socially awkward and had trouble connecting with my peers. I wanted desperately to be like the "cool kids" but found them insufferable and uncomfortable to be around. I sought to be a peacekeeper, finding ways to ease conflict and eliminate fighting where possible. My dreams about the future centered on traveling and helping people in need. There was no discernable occupation attached to my dreams because I wasn't aware of a job that appealed to my personality. I completed high school and went to college without a clue of what I wanted to be when I "grew up."

Genesis 1:26-28 (KJV) *– And God said, Let us make man in our image, after our likeness: and let them have dominion over the fish of the sea, and over the fowl of the air, and over the cattle, and over all the earth, and over every creeping thing that creepeth upon the earth.*

The book of Genesis speaks of God creating man (and woman) in God's own image, and by virtue of that fact, it stands to reason that humans were created as whole and complete beings. Humans created in the image and likeness of God also indicate that there is nothing lacking in their personhood. With this completeness came the agency and authority to have dominion over the other things that God created – the fish, fowl, cattle, and other creeping things. God charged humans to be good stewards of the earth and trusted them to do what was necessary to promote growth and flourishing in the new creation.

As children, we are born with an internal flame that helps to guide us throughout our existence. This light animates our imagination, illuminates the path that we ultimately take, and provides rationale and reasoning for what we do. Whether we are jumping up and down on the bed, eating cookies from the cookie jar, or annoying our parents to no end, we are acting in accordance with who we know ourselves to be. It is during the formative childhood years – the times of coming to know ourselves – that we are introduced to life's lessons, contradictions, and challenges. For many, this period of formation leads to a state of confusion that takes a lifetime to understand.

It is during these early years that we are shaped, nurtured, and shepherded through life. Parents, grandparents, teachers, mentors, and others fill our heads with their understanding of what we need to do and how we need to operate to become successful in life. The lessons and best well-intentioned teachings of those who love us often have the effect of forcing us to look outside of ourselves for the answers to life's many questions. As one who has taken this arduous journey myself, I can say that the best intentions of loved ones kickstarted me on a journey of growth, discovery, change, and transformation. This important journey, once completed, becomes the essential journey to self-awareness and understanding.

My essential journey began on the campus of the Alabama State University in Montgomery, Alabama. During my time there, I battled with the multiple identities that were inside of me, including the personality I had taken on to satisfy what was expected of me and the person who really was – the me that was trying to break free. I didn't know it at the time, but no amount of conformity – and no amount of self-suppression – could eliminate the passions and desires residing deep inside of my being.

Romans 12:2 (KJV) – *And be not conformed to this world: but be ye transformed by the renewing of your mind, that ye may prove what is that good, and acceptable, and perfect will of God.*

In our youth, we are shaped and molded by images, examples, and expressions that are deemed acceptable – and successful – in the eyes of society. Thoughtful and caring adults do their best to prepare us for the "real world" and unwittingly collude with advertising agencies, marketing executives, television studios, movie producers, and social media influencers – leading us away from our true passions and toward a life of respectable conformity. In doing so, the internal flames of individuality are extinguished, and young and impressionable souls contort themselves into what is culturally acceptable – all the while abandoning what makes them truly unique. Or maybe that's just my story.

Even in its most subtle form, our cultural and familial influences change how we see and perceive ourselves. We modify our behavior to be liked, desired, or to make others proud. We are conditioned from birth to perform so that we are praised and not punished. In the short-term, conforming will work on some levels – social acceptance and favorable treatment – but the long-standing ramifications tend to kill what is inside: the passion and purpose of the individual.

In Romans 12:2, the Apostle Paul admonishes readers to "not be conformed to the world…" Bible readers will know that Paul is one who spoke from the authority of his experiences and possessed both the practical and philosophical gravitas to make a statement this bold. I remember this scripture hitting me differently when I was in a place of seeking during my journey to myself.

Wrestling with questions of identity and purpose led me to adopt Romans 12:2 as one of my foundational scriptures, and I subsequently incorporated it into my life philosophy. This is when I began to notice that my life was starting to change. I started earnestly seeking and searching for my true my raison d'etre, and this led me to the greatest discovery of my life: that which I was seeking was inside of me. I needed to go back to where I had lost myself.

2 Kings 6:5-6 (NLT) – But as one of them was cutting a tree, his ax head fell into the river. "Oh, sir!" he cried. "It was a borrowed ax!" "Where did it fall?" the man of God asked. When he showed him the place, Elisha cut a stick and threw it into the water at that spot. Then the ax head floated to the surface.

The greatest discovery of my life came not from a place of foreign origin, but a place that I was thoroughly unfamiliar with –

the inside of me. I realized that I had spent the majority of my life seeking and striving to attain and obtain external treasures, while all that I needed was waiting to be uncovered and not discovered. After years of schooling, experiences, assignments, career changes, degrees, certificates, and other accolades, I found myself empty and impotent. I had not sufficiently fed my passions, nor my person and my spirit man hungered. Like the man of God in 2 Kings 6, I was instructed to return to the place where I lost my ax – and that was to the will of God. I was reminded of the invitation to take God at God's word and the promise that was made to me. I appreciated everyone who offered support, care, and comfort, but I had to return to the one who created, called, and commissioned me – the Lord God almighty. Much like Paul in Romans 12:2, John's writing in Revelation 3:20 hit differently this time:

Revelation 3:20 (KJV) *– "Behold, I stand at the door, and knock: if any man hears my voice, and open the door, I will come to him, and will sup with him, and he with me."*

I was reminded that God had never left me. I understood how slowly – throughout the years – I had been indoctrinated into a culture of conformity and chaos. The more I tried to please people, the still, small voice inside was drowned out by ambition and accomplishments. I can still remember me crying out to God in a state of desperation and hopelessness – "God, you've got to have more for me than this… whatever you want me to do, I'll do; wherever you want me to go, I'll go!"

That was the beginning of me waking up from the coma of conformity and entering into the state of eternal understanding. God said, "Let us make man in our image, after our likeness: and let them have dominion (Genesis 1:26)". The world had confused my thinking; I mistakenly had let the world have dominion over me. Once this confusion was corrected, I began to see how the God inside of me was seeking expression in my life. Since I reconnected with God – the God who is living within me – I have been amazed at what God has done in and through me. When we finally make the essential journey, we come back to the place where it all started: ourselves.

When God called me to service in New Jersey, I was afraid, apprehensive, and amazed. I was afraid of starting over again. I was apprehensive because of identity issues and uncertainty. And somehow, while I was afraid and apprehensive, I was simultaneously amazed at God's faithfulness and dedication to me in spite of my flawed humanity. Eight years after arriving in the Garden State, God's calling and commission could not be more evident in my life. The internal flame that was barely a flicker when I arrived, has become a towering flame that has helped ignite the candles in thousands of people, ministries, and organizations over the years.

When we accept Jesus into our lives and hearts, it means that God has taken up residence with us and we have allowed God to have dominion over us. The Holy Spirit making his dwelling inside of our bodies is a constant companion and source of power, might, and transformation. Those who truly live a transformed life will cite their acceptance of Jesus as the turning point in their existence. There is a noticeable difference to their character, behavior, and ultimate impact. Listening to such people, you will find that the after is full of life, adventure, and new-ness. There is a sense of freedom and fearlessness that accompanies this new life all because God is now living within – or more accurately – was there the entire time.

I praise God for the freedom granted to me. It hit me: This is not just a freedom from pain or brokenness, it's also freedom from conformity. I began to think about the fact that no matter what I am called to do, I am free to do it. There are no chains holding me to a specific box or mold. Whatever dreams God downloads into my spirit, I can do. John 8:36 paraphrased informs us that who the Son sets free, is free indeed. I am free to think, to imagine, act and to do – because the God of the universe lives and dwells within me. One of the most powerful lessons that came out of the essential journey – my journey to me – is that for God to restore you, there will be an interruption. Although I didn't appreciate it at the time, I thank God for divine interruptions. It is because the divine interruptions allowed me the opportunity to refocus on the prize – the prize that lives inside. All praises belong to God!

Len Wood

Reflections of the Spirit Within

Reflections of the Spirit Within

Not spirit from a can
Or an MP3
Just plain old words on paper Eventually keyed into a computer
Using Microsoft Word

Describing what is going on inside
Describing what the spirits are brewing
The inner vocalization of the spirit's stew
Screaming in all CAPS as though
Written loudly in BLUE and GREEN

Transitioning through hues from all blues to green
The SPIRIT gets you through those blues
It becomes Nueva Verde
The New Green--a re-greening

A Re-birth inside that happens everyday
This is the spirit inside all of us
The SPIRIT within we call God
The HE or SHE also known as Buddha, Allah, Coke or Pepsi
Or whatever else we call our higher being
Or whatever else we call it
When our being is higher
Perhaps lower
When we end up inside ourselves
We reach this Magic Moment
When we are jolted and ask Big Spirit
Why did this happen?

Why did this happen to me?
It is usually the way many of us learn to pray
The blue period continues
And the hole gets deeper

And our prayers get a little deeper
And a little stronger
We scream

We pull our hair out
WE CRY
God why the XXXX is this continuing to happen to me?
Why my Big Friend in the Sky?
Is this real?

This cannot be happening to me again
When will this XXXX stop?
We sit down at the table by ourselves
We begin this conversation with our Spirit
Suddenly this storm blows over
It could have been years, months, days or just minutes
The clouds disappear
That is the moment of the miracle
Was it the prayer?
The time we dug in to call on the Spirit Within?
Call it that little bit of God inside
Call it anything you want
The Spirit sits inside all of us waiting to be called
When the world around us
And inside us-- needs to stop for a moment

It is as Mr. Wonder said
If you think that life's too hard
Just go have a talk with God
Just start a conversation
We ask ourselves
Where do I go from here?
How do I get there from here?
To Peace, Love and Understanding
One more time please
How do we get to here?
To Peace, Love and Understanding
To find the Spirit
We must first find the love inside ourselves

Forgive and let go of the baggage
Of those feelings we have about our neighbors and our past
We can then forgive ourselves
For being what we are
And Others for being who they are

The Spirit Within is that warm blanket
Covering the shoulders of our souls
When we are cold and lonely
When there is no place to go
When we crawl into a corner
Feeling beaten and humbled
Afraid, without direction
We wrap the blanket tighter
As the chill and wind go through us

The fear subsides as the Spirit spreads love
From head to toe
Throughout our bodies
Enveloping us with an invincibility Of a Spirit filled with love
This Spirit Within cures the Spirit Without
We don't need to write a check

No need to go the ATM
No security deposit required
The Spirit Within cures all
Rest your head gently in your hands
Let the Spirit Within do the work
Let the miracle begin!

Contributors

ELMAZ ABINADER is an author and a performer. Her most recent poetry collection, This House, My Bones, was The Editor's Selection for 2014 from Willow Books/Aquarius. Her books include a memoir: Children of the Roojme, A Family's Journey from Lebanon, a book of poetry, In the Country of My Dreams... which won the Oakland PEN, Josephine Miles Award.

Recently she was awarded a Trailblazer Award by RAWI (Radius of Arab Writers International). Her plays include Ramadan Moon, 32 Mohammeds, and Country of Origin. She has been a frequent contributor to Al-Jazeera English. She has been anthologized widely including the New Anthology of American Poetry, and in The Colors of Nature. She has been a fellow at residencies in Marfa (Lannan) Macedonia, Brazil, Spain and Egypt and a Senior Fulbright Fellow. Her teaching includes Master Workshops for Hedgebrook in India as well as for VORTEXT.

Elmaz is one of the co-founders of The Voices of Our Nations Arts Foundation (VONA/Voices) a writing workshop for writers-of-color. She teaches at Mills College and the University of San Francisco.

DEBRA BARSHA hopscotches "across the boundaries of contemporary music. Gleefully defying classification, Barsha is that rare talent that sees show business itself as a medium. Singer, songwriter, actress, composer, pianist, raconteur, Barsha is just as comfortable fueling the grooves on a George Clinton album as she is composing the score of an off-Broadway musical about pop-art icon Keith Haring (RADIANT BABY). She is also a founding member of the Equanimity Band. With a career that includes television soundtracks, one-woman shows, children's musicals and international tours with post-mod British pop-stars (Thomas

Dolby), Barsha manages to put the undeniable stamp of her own musical personality on the full spectrum of her work."

FRANK COLON is a specialist in Latin-Caribbean, Brazilian and Asian percussion instruments including congas, bongos, timbales, bata drums, shekere, cuica, berimbau, and tabla drums, among others. Frank began his musical career with a five-year stint in Julito Collazo's Afro-Cuban drum ensemble. On NYC's jazz scene, he quickly went on to perform and record with Walter Booker, Chet Baker, Jaco Pastorious, Michel Camilo, African master drummer, Babatunde Olatunji, Gato Barbieri, Harry Belafonte, Weather Report, Tania Maria, Flora Purim, and Airto Moreira.

In Brazil, Frank has also performed and/or recorded with Milton Nascimento, Gilberto Gil, Motta, João Bosco, Chico Buarque, Wagner Tiso, Ney Matogrosso, Elba Ramalho, Marina Lima, RPM, João Donato, Toninho Horta, Roberto Menescal, and Marcos Valle.

As a sideman with the Manhattan Transfer for 12 years, he participated on two of their Grammy-winning records and was voted in 1988 as one of the top three "Most Influential Percussionist of the Year" in the Modern Drummer Magazine poll!

His three albums as a leader are: "Frank Colón - Live at Vartanjazz", "Latin Wonder", and "Latin Lounge", all of which have received very good critical reviews. He is also featured as the principal soloist in a DVD by the Russian String Orchestra from Moscow, in a symphony commissioned for him entitled "Adoracion al Ritmo."

CHARLES "CHUCK" CUYJET is a happily retired leadership and career coach, living in Northern Virginia with his wife, his daughter, and two cats. He's probably off somewhere riding his bicycle right now.

PHERALYN DOVE is a word-warrior: poet, writer, educator. She lives in a state of perpetual gratitude. A graduate of Hampton University, she is the author of "Color in Motion, a book of poetry with a foreword by drummer Max Roach. Little Girl Blue, her one-woman show in which she portrays 17 characters, is a multi-media production about a woman's journey from victim to victor. She performed at Jazz a la Villette in Paris and was chosen for the juried NYC International Fringe Fest. She is featured on bassist Tyrone Brown's, Moon of the Falling Leaves CD.

KEITA ERSKINE is a New York based writer, slam poet, activist and journalist. He studied journalism at Northwestern University and works as a researcher and contract strategist.

FRANCESCO GARRI GARRIPOLI is the Chairman of the Board of the Qigong Institute and is an author, Senior Qigong Teacher Certified with the National Qigong Association and wellness advocate. He began his formal training in Eastern healing in Hawaii in 1977 after leaving a full medical school scholarship. An Emmy Award-winning producer, his documentary "Qigong: Ancient Chinese Healing for the 21st Century" produced for PBS Television, was seen by 88 million viewers. Francesco teaches Qigong and meditation workshops and Instructor Certification trainings around the world. He is Chairman Emeritus of the National Qigong Association, author of Qigong Essence of the Healing Dance and Tao of the Ride and founded the non-profit CommunityAwake to further explorations in Qigong and personal transformation.

ARCHIE IVY is a music industry executive, who has spent over 40 years bringing innovations and new insights to international audiences, as General Director and key advisor of George Clinton Enterprises. Additionally, Archie is an ordained Pentecostal Minister and co-founder of an outreach ministry in Tallahassee Florida. Rev. Ivy is matriculated from UCLA and Antioch University.

MARC A. KLINE is the rabbi at the Temple Ohev Sholom in Harrisburg, Pennsylvania. Ordained in 1995, his deeply rooted faith and love for Torah is based upon his passion for tradition and social justice. Prior to his study at Hebrew Union College (seminary), where he earned his Master of Arts in Hebrew Letters and Doctor of Divinity degrees, Rabbi Kline received his Juris Doctor from the University of Arkansas at Little Rock and practiced law there for almost 6 years. Happily married to Lori Bernard, he is a father and grandfather.

J. D. PARRAN is a multi-woodwind player, educator, and composer specializing in jazz and free improvised music. He has recorded with Stevie Wonder, John Lennon and is a member of the Equanimity Band. He attended Webster University and received an M.A. in music education from Washington University in St. Louis.

CAROL A. PENN, DO, MA, ABOM, FACOFP is triply Board Certified in Family Medicine and Obesity Medicine as well as being a Master movement, meditation, and mindset coach brings more than 40 years of experience and expertise in Mind Body Medicine and the movement sciences. Gifted with the ability to inspire and educate about self-care, Dr. Penn brings a unique set of skills to her work as a physician. She is also a three-time best-selling author and her book and journal series: Meditation in a Time of Madness, launched in 2019 as a #1 Best Seller in the category of meditation and alternative medicine.

Dr. Carol, hoping to guide each person on their own unique journey, integrates her background as a professionally trained dancer and choreographer, with the world-famous Alvin Ailey American Dance Theater and a Kennedy Center for the Performing Arts Teaching Fellow, will get you moving and keep you moving on your path to health and wellness.

A businesswoman, servant leader and entrepreneur, Dr. Penn is a Founder/Activist and Chief Visionary Officer of Penn Global Visions LLC, and Chief Medical Officer of Penn Global Medical Group. Fondly known as the Dean of Spiritual Legacy, on WURD's Envy McKee show, she is a frequent guest and Podcastor as well as the host of her own weekly show and podcast: Weightless in Mind,

Body and Spirit. A creative forever, she continues to direct her all volunteer women's dance ensemble Core of Fire.

AMY SHIMSHON-SANTO is a writer and educator who believes that creativity is a powerful tool for personal and social transformation. Her work connects the arts, education, and urbanism. Dr. Shimsohn-Santo's books include Milky Way, Endless Bowls of Sky and Alphabet Quest.

Amy has enjoyed a fulfilling career teaching and learning locally and internationally. She currently offers public workshops for communities, coaches individuals and teams, and provides graduate level instruction in the arts, culture, and education.

Amy's commitment to teaching and learning is rooted in community arts practice. Early in her career, she developed curriculum and educational programming for the Brasil Brasil Cultural Center, and reached communities through workshops and performances throughout California, the United States, and abroad. Her educational projects earned support from the California Arts Council, the Irvine Foundation, Los Angeles Division of Cultural Affairs, the National Endowment for the Arts, and national recognition on the Presidential Honor Roll for Service Learning.

Amy has mentored young leaders in higher education at the undergraduate, Masters, and Doctoral levels of study. She served as Associate Professor and directed the M.A. in Arts Management Program that included developing community partnerships and designing global study programming in Africa, Latin America, Asia, and the Middle East. Prior to that, she directed the Artsbridge Program at UCLA Arts where she taught for seven years serving as the UCLA Arts liaison to the Graduate School of Education and Information Sciences, spearheading a dance credential and coaching teachers. Her work connected emerging artists with students and teaching in LAUSD, Compton USD, Lynwood USD, Santa Monica USD and the University of California. Her work lay the groundwork for the first Visual and Performing Arts Education degree (VAPAE Minor) in the UC system earning a state commendation from the Governor of California. Later, Amy served as a Visiting Scholar for the Center for Learning Through the Arts, Sciences, and Sustainability (CLASS) at UC Irvine where she studied public policy issues related to arts education while teaching courses for the Department of Education.

TOUSSIANT L is the grandson of a woman evangelist and a deacon raised in the Black Baptist Church. He is an open-minded unapologetic Christian. He lives life seeing miracles with God's grace. Toussaint acknowledges all and those who choose to believe there is a higher power whatever name you call your higher power he calls God.

MONA R. WASHINGTON is a librettist and playwright, as well as an attorney.

KERWIN WEBB serves as Youth and Young Adult Pastor at Second Baptist Church of Asbury Park and the President of the Greater Red Bank Area NAACP. A native of Birmingham, Rev. Webb earned a bachelor's degree in Business Administration from Alabama State University in 2004. Kerwin's passions include education, mentoring, training, and community development – and so, he founded RMW Foundation, Inc. in 2013. He is currently employed as the Education Specialist for Interfaith Neighbors in Asbury Park. Rev. Kerwin hopes his continued work with individuals, churches, and community organizations will led to transformation and change within both individuals and communities.

Recognized guitar maker LEN WOOD began his relationship with instrument construction at the age of 7. After studying Business at Babson, Wood was working for Intel in the Philippines when he decided to integrate his business-sense with his passion for art. Apprenticing at a nearby guitar factory, an old guitar maker took him under his wing. For months Wood spent hours daily learning the methods and craft of guitar building, resulting in a career that would feature his instruments in the Smithsonian and in the hands of music legends such as Wah Wah Watson. Len is a master of musical improvisation and is the music director of the Equanimity Band.

Although Wood eventually made his way back to the United

States, he maintained his ties with the Philippines and started a company, the Custom Guitar Company, that manufactures abalone and mother of pearl blanks for inlay. Renowned by luthiers for his meticulous attention to quality, the product of a scrutinous hand-selection process, the materials ornament a wide range of products, from instruments to furniture.

Wood is also known as C.M.M. throughout his travels: Chief Mischief Maker.

About Diem Jones

DIEM JONES is a thought leader, writer, poet/musician, multi-disciplinary producer, and program designer, and believes in Cultural Consciousness through the integration of poetry and broad-based diasporic music. His publications include #1 Bimini Road, Sufi Warrior, A Big Day: Thawing the Soul and is published in numerous anthologies and has three solo CD's Black Fish Jazz, Equanimity and A Spirit of Oui. In addition to having directed creative writing programs on 6 US university campuses, his work as a producer has won critical acclaim in: music videos, industrial films, and documentaries as well as commercials. He is currently the COO of Penn Global Visions and CEO of All One Consulting. He is co-founder and past Executive Director of Voices of Our Nations Arts Foundation (VONA/Voices).

Additionally, Jones is past Executive Director of Murray Grove Retreat Center and Creative Director of George Clinton and Parliament Funkadelic. His recent single, "Sub-Atomic God" produced by Equanimity Music and We Baad Tribe Entertainment and released in early 2022, is an inspirational motivational danceable song created with Amp Fiddler.

An accomplished photographer and art director, Diem Jones produced over 60 album covers, and created some of the most controversial album covers in music history." He is forever committed to Funk, Soul, and Love. He received his Bachelor of Arts degree in filmmaking from American University, where he completed graduate studies in Broadcast Management.